the
SLOW COOKER
bible

super simple feasts for the whole family

with recipes from Sara Lewis,
Saskia Sidey and Libby Silbermann

An Hachette UK Company
www.hachette.co.uk

First published in Great Britain in 2021 by Pyramid,
an imprint of Octopus Publishing Group Ltd
Carmelite House
50 Victoria Embankment
London EC4Y 0DZ
www.octopusbooks.co.uk

ISBN 978-0-7537-3492-6

A CIP catalogue record for this book is available from
the British Library.

Printed and bound in China

10 9 8 7 6 5 4 3 2 1

Publisher: Lucy Pessell
Designer: Hannah Coughlin
Junior Editor: Sarah Kennedy
Editorial Assistant: Emily Martin
Contributing Authors: Sara Lewis,
Saskia Sidey and Libby Silbermann
Contributing Editor: Jane Birch
Production Manager: Caroline Alberti
Photography © Octopus Publishing Group
Limited/Stephen Conroy, William Shaw

Cook's Notes

Standard level spoon measures are used in all recipes:
1 tablespoon = one 15 ml spoon
1 teaspoon = one 5 ml spoon

Both metric and imperial measurements are given
for the recipes. Use one set of measures only, not a
mixture of both.

Medium eggs have been used throughout.

Fresh herbs should be used unless otherwise stated.

A few recipes contain nuts and nut derivatives.
Anyone with a known nut allergy must avoid these.

This book contains some dishes made with raw or
lightly cooked eggs. It is prudent for more vulnerable
people such as pregnant and nursing mothers, the
elderly, babies and young children to avoid raw or
lightly cooked eggs.

Ovens should be preheated to the specific
temperature – if using a fan-assisted oven, follow
the manufacturer's instructions for adjusting the
time and the temperature.

Read your slow cooker manual before you begin and
preheat the slow cooker if required according to the
manufacturer's instructions. Because slow cookers vary
slightly from manufacturer to manufacturer, check
recipe timings with the manufacturer's directions for
a recipe using the same ingredients.

All recipes for this book were tested in oval-shaped
slow cookers with a working capacity of 2.5 litres
(4 pints) and total capacity of 3.5 litres (6 pints)
using metric measurements.

Where the slow cooker recipe is finished off under the
grill, hold the pot with tea towels to remove it from
the machine housing.

Contents

Introduction

Introduction

Whether you are new to slow cooking or a seasoned pro, you probably have a handful of favourite recipes that you keep going back to. It's true that some classics taste absolutely delicious when slow cooked, time after time: lamb stews, beef casseroles, coq au vin.

But a slow cooker isn't just for casseroles and stews, great though they are. You can make a huge variety of other dishes, including lighter meals, delicious fish recipes and hearty vegetarian and vegan dishes. Try warming breakfasts such as overnight turmeric porridge, or delicious soups like corn and smoked cod chowder, or a vegetable-packed spinach and courgette tian.

It may sound contradictory, but slow cooking is quick and easy. All you have to do is prepare and add your ingredients to the pot; there's no constant stirring involved or having to stand over a stove. It's also cheaper – not only can you make the most of more-affordable root vegetables, slow cookers also use less energy than other cooking methods, saving you even more money on your bills.

How to use this book

In this book you will find a wide range of recipes that are perfect for any occasion. Whether you're looking for a meal that is easy to put together and ready to eat in under three-and-a-half hours, or if you're looking for something to put together in the mornings ready for when you're back from work. You will also find delicious vegetarian and vegan meals, as well as lighter options. Each recipe has a symbol to help you pick the perfect meal – vegetarian options are marked with V, Vegan options with VE, gluten free with GF. dairy-free options with DF and lighter options with L.

Some of the recipes in this book also include variations at the bottom of the page for when you want to mix it up a little or perhaps swap out an ingredient depending on what you have in your cupboards.

Slow cooking basics

Choosing a slow cooker

All slow cookers cook food slowly, though they do vary slightly. Oval-shaped slow cookers offer the most flexibility when it comes to cooking joints or desserts. Generally, slow cookers come in three sizes:

- a two-portion size with a capacity of 1.5 litres (2 pints)
- a four-portion size with a capacity of 2.5 litres (4 pints)
- a six-to-eight portion size with a capacity of 4 litres (7 pints) or 4.5 litres (8 pints).

Newer models might come with cooking pots that can be used on the hob, so you can fry off meat and onions prior to slow cooking in the slow cooker pot itself, saving on washing up. These types of slow cookers do tend to cost more. A good non-stick frying pan in conjunction with a slow cooker works just as well.

As with all things, price varies considerably. The larger models are very often on special offer, but unless your family is large or you plan to cook larger quantities in order to freeze half of the batch, you may find that, while the machine itself is a good price, you have to cook larger quantities than you had expected in order to just half-fill it.

When selecting a slow cooker, choose a machine with a high and low setting and an on/off light at the front of the machine so that you can see easily that it is on. There is nothing more frustrating than to come back eight hours later, expecting a hot, delicious meal, only to find that you haven't turned the machine on! Some models have a setting that allows you to keep the food warm, which is useful. Digital clocks are great, but they are certainly not essential.

Dull though it sounds, once you've purchased a slow cooker, make sure you read the handbook. The majority of models should not be preheated with an empty slow cooker pot. If you part-prep supper the night before and put the earthenware slow cooker pot in the refrigerator, all manufacturers agree that you should leave it at room temperature for 20 minutes before adding it to the slow cooker machine and turning it on.

Is it safe to leave the slow cooker on all day?

Yes – the slow cooker runs on such a small amount of power (the equivalent of two light bulbs) that it is safe to leave it on all day – even if you go out. Because the heat is so low and the lid forms a seal, there is no danger of the food boiling dry. The sides of the slow cooker will feel warm to the touch, so ensure you leave the machine on a non-cluttered part of the work surface.

Do I need to fry food before adding it to the slow cooker pot?

Frying onions and browning meat adds colour and flavour to the finished dish, but it isn't essential – it's very much a matter of personal taste. If you don't fry off your ingredients beforehand, you may end up with something a little less tasty, but still delicious all the same.

Does liquid have to be hot before going into the slow cooker pot?

The slow cooker works by building up heat to just below boiling point, then safely maintaining the heat so that food cooks gently but without any danger of allowing the bacteria that cause food poisoning to proliferate. If you add all cold ingredients, this will obviously extend the heating-up process, so add 2–3 hours to the cooking time, with the first hour on high, especially if the recipe states to use hot stock. But it is much quicker and very simple to dissolve a stock cube in boiling water and add the hot stock to the slow cooker pot. Always add hot liquid when cooking large joints.

How full should the pot be?

Ideally, the slow cooker pot should be filled half full and up to three-quarters full for it to work efficiently. For soups, fill it so that the liquid is 5 cm (2 inches) from the top. If you have a very large slow cooker, make up amounts to serve six to eight people, then freeze the extra in single portions or portion sizes that will suit your family on another day.

There seems to be a lot of water around the lid – is this okay?

Yes perfectly – as the slow cooker comes up to temperature the steam condenses and forms a seal around the lid. Every time you lift the lid you break the seal and add an extra 20 minutes to the cooking time. Resist the temptation to lift the lid more than is absolutely necessary. It takes the slow cooker 1 hour to come up to a safe and optimal temperature.

How will I know the food is ready and cooked-through?

This is particularly crucial when cooking meat and fish, but especially when cooking joints. Test as you would if cooking in a conventional oven by inserting a knife into the centre, or through the thickest part of the leg, or into the breast if testing a whole chicken. The juices that run out should be clear with no hint of pink and the tip of the knife should feel hot. The knife will also slide into meat easily if tender. For smaller chunks or cubes of meat, take a piece out, cut in half and, if done, taste for tenderness.

When testing chicken or duck portions or lamb shanks, the meat will begin to shrink away from the bone when tender; as with the larger joints, press a knife into the thickest part of the joint. Fish should break easily into even-coloured flakes when pressed in the centre with a knife.

For extra piece of mind, a digital meat probe can be a fail-safe way to check, as it will tell you exactly the internal temperature of the meat.

Top tips

- The smaller the pieces of food, the quicker they will cook.
- Food at the bottom of the slow cooker pot will cook more quickly so put root vegetables into the pot first.
- Don't worry if you get delayed, the food will be fine for an extra hour or so.
- Resist the temptation to take the lid off during cooking. Every time you remove the lid the slow cooker will lose heat, and you will end up waiting longer for your food to cook through.

Getting the most out of your slow cooker

Using your slow cooker for the first time

Before you start to use the slow cooker, put it on the work surface, somewhere out of the way and make sure that the flex is tucked around the back of the machine and not trailing over the front of the work surface.

The outside of the slow cooker does get hot, so warn young members of the family. Don't forget to wear oven gloves or use tea towels when you are lifting the pot out of the housing, and always place the pot on a heatproof mat on the table or work surface to serve the food.

Don't put your slow cooker under an eye-level cupboard if the lid has a vent in the top. The steam from the vent could burn someone's arm as they reach into the cupboard.

Always check that the joint, pudding basin, soufflé dish or individual moulds will fit into your slow cooker pot before you begin work on a recipe to avoid frustration when you get to a critical point.

Caring for your slow cooker

Because a slow cooker heats food to a lower heat than a conventional oven there are no burnt-on splashes or stubborn marks to get rid of. At the end of cooking, remove the empty earthenware pot from the slow cooker, fill it with warm soapy water and leave to soak, if necessary, then remove any marks with a washing-up brush. Don't stand the pot in water – the unglazed areas are porous and so will soak up water and could then possibly crack when heated in the slow cooker. Some pots are dishwasher safe, but not all, so check with your instruction handbook first.

Wipe out the inside of the slow cooker machine with a damp cloth and a squirt of cream cleanser, making sure that it is unplugged first. Buff up the outside with a dry cloth. Never immerse in water.

Removing a basin from the slow cooker

So that you can easily lift a hot basin out of the slow cooker, tear off two long pieces of foil. Fold each into thirds to make a long, thin strap. Put one on top of the other to make a cross, then sit the pudding basin in the centre. Lift up the straps, then lower the basin into the slow cooker pot carefully. Use the straps to remove the basin at the end of cooking.

Safety tips

- Always read the instruction handbook that accompanies your slow cooker before you begin.
- Make sure frozen food is completely defrosted before adding it to the slow cooker, with the exception of a small quantity of frozen peas or sweetcorn towards the end of cooking, or frozen fruit.
- Add hot liquid or stock to the slow cooker pot; this is especially important if the meat is not fried first.
- Don't lift the lid off the slow cooker during the first hour of cooking while the slow cooker heats up to a safe and optimal temperature.
- If a recipe requires you to lift dishes out of the slow cooker pot, use a tea towel or foil straps (see below).
- The outside of the slow cooker housing gets hot when in use – use oven gloves if removing the pot from the housing as soon as cooking has finished.
- Never reheat already cooked food in a slow cooker.
- Don't leave cooked food to cool down in the turned off slow cooker.

Breakfasts

PB & J French Toast Bake

Blueberry & Cinnamon French Toast

Honey, Nut & Seed Granola

Cherry Bakewell Breakfast Cake

Seedy Banana Breakfast Loaf

Banana & Cinnamon Porridge

Overnight Turmeric Porridge

Brunch Poached Eggs & Haddock

Baked Eggs with Toast

Eggs en Cocotte with Salmon

Shakshuka

Tofu Shakshuka

Smoky Breakfast Beans

Baked Peppers with Chorizo

Easy Sausage & Beans

Sweet Potato, Goats' Cheese & Thyme Frittata

Toffee Apple Pancakes

PB & J French Toast Bake

Take the base formula for this French toast bake and experiment with different flavour combinations – swap the peanut butter and jam for melted vegan chocolate or go down the savoury route with some vegan cheese.

Serves 4
Preparation time 15 minutes, plus standing
Cooking temperature high
Cooking time 1–1½ hours

½ tablespoon sunflower or vegetable oil, for greasing

2 tablespoons ground flaxseed

50 g (2 oz) vegan butter, melted

200 ml (7 fl oz) unsweetened almond milk

3 tablespoons smooth peanut butter

½ teaspoon ground cinnamon

¼ teaspoon ground nutmeg

½ teaspoon baking powder

250 g (8 oz) stale sourdough, cut into large cubes

To serve

icing sugar

3 tablespoons jam of your choice or Blueberry Jam (below)

roasted, unsalted peanuts, roughly chopped

Preheat the slow cooker if necessary. Grease the slow cooker pot with the oil.

Put the ground flaxseed, melted vegan butter, almond milk, peanut butter and spices into the slow cooker, use a whisk to break up the peanut butter and whisk until the mixture is emulsified. Leave to stand for 5–10 minutes until slightly thickened.

Stir in the baking powder, add the bread cubes and toss until well coated in the mixture.

Place a tea towel or kitchen paper underneath the slow cooker lid, cover the cooker and cook on high for 1–1½ hours until springy but firm to the touch and the remaining liquid is thickened, golden and bubbly.

Serve immediately, dusted with icing sugar, drizzled with jam – try the Homemade Blueberry Jam (see below), if you like – and scattered with chopped roasted peanuts.

For homemade blueberry jam, to serve as an accompaniment, put 500 g (1 lb) fresh blueberries, 4 tablespoons lemon juice and 2 tablespoons water in a large saucepan and cook gently for about 8–10 minutes until the blueberries are soft. Stir in 450 g (14½ oz) preserving or granulated sugar and heat gently until the sugar dissolves. Bring to the boil and boil for 10–15 minutes until setting point is reached. Ladle into sterilized jars, put the lids on and label.

Blueberry & Cinnamon French Toast

French toast is a great weekend treat. This cinnamon-spiced version with blueberries is delicious served warm and drizzled with honey, alongside thick Greek yogurt and plenty of coffee.

Serves 4
Preparation time 15 minutes, plus overnight soaking
Cooking temperature low
Cooking time 4 hours

50 g (2 oz) butter, softened, plus extra for greasing

1 teaspoon ground cinnamon

150 g (5 oz) soft brown sugar, plus extra for sprinkling

8 slices of bread, slightly stale

1 teaspoon vanilla bean paste

pinch of sea salt

3 large eggs

300 ml (½ pint) milk

100 g (3½ oz) blueberries, plus extra to serve

To serve
natural Greek yogurt
clear honey

Beat together the butter, cinnamon and sugar in a small bowl until it forms a smooth paste, then carefully spread each slice of bread with the butter mixture on both sides.

Whisk together the vanilla, salt, eggs and milk in a large, shallow dish until smooth. Place the slices of bread into the egg mixture, ensuring each slice is submerged. Cover the dish with clingfilm and place in the refrigerator overnight.

When ready to cook, preheat the slow cooker if necessary. Grease the slow cooker pot well with butter. Arrange a layer of the soaked bread slices in the bottom of the pot. Sprinkle over a layer of blueberries, then add another layer of bread. Repeat until all the bread and blueberries are used, then pour over any remaining egg mixture and sprinkle the top with sugar.

Cover with the lid and cook on low for 4 hours until the egg mixture has thickened and set. Carefully remove the slow cooker pot from the slow cooker using oven gloves. Loosen the edge of the French toast with a knife, and turn out onto a large plate. Cut into slices and serve with dollops of yogurt, extra blueberries and a drizzle of honey.

Honey, Nut & Seed Granola

(DF) (V)

This recipe is brilliant for making and storing a large batch of granola. The nuts, seeds and dried fruit are easily changeable, so experiment and try different flavour combinations.

Serves 12
Preparation time 10 minutes, plus cooling
Cooking temperature high
Cooking time 2½ hours

350 g (11½ oz) jumbo oats

100 g (3½ oz) coconut flakes

50 g (2 oz) sunflower seeds

50 g (2 oz) almonds, chopped

50 g (2 oz) walnuts, chopped

1 teaspoon ground cinnamon

4 tablespoons coconut oil, melted

180 g (6 oz) clear honey or agave syrup

50 ml (2 fl oz) water

1 teaspoon vanilla extract

120 g (4 oz) raisins

50 g (2 oz) dried cranberries

Preheat the slow cooker if necessary. Put the oats, coconut flakes, seeds, nuts and cinnamon into the slow cooker and mix well.

Mix together the coconut oil, honey or agave syrup, measured water and vanilla in a small bowl, then pour over the oat mixture and stir until well combined.

Cover with the lid at a slight angle so there is a small gap to allow the steam to escape (this will help the granola to crisp), then cook on high for 2½ hours, stirring gently every 40 minutes to ensure the mixture is not sticking to the pot or burning.

Carefully remove the slow cooker pot from the slow cooker using oven gloves, then carefully tip the granola into a large baking tray and spread it out evenly. Leave to cool (this ensures it will be crunchy), then stir in the raisins and cranberries. Store in an airtight container for up to 2 weeks.

Serve the granola with yogurt and fresh berries, or simply with your milk of choice.

Cherry Bakewell Breakfast Cake

 VE

This is the closest you can get to eating dessert for breakfast without feeling guilty. Swap the dried cherries for other dried fruit of your choice, such as raisins, sultanas, dried cranberries or roughly chopped dried apricots, or try fresh cherries, raspberries or blackberries when in season.

Makes 6–8 slices
Preparation time 15 minutes
Cooking temperature high
Cooking time 1–1½ hours

70 ml (2½ fl oz) melted coconut, vegetable or sunflower oil
200 ml (7 fl oz) unsweetened almond milk
finely grated rind and juice of 1 unwaxed lemon
120 ml (4 fl oz) maple syrup
1 teaspoon vanilla bean paste
½ teaspoon salt
150 g (5 oz) ground almonds
150 g (5 oz) self-raising flour
½ teaspoon bicarbonate of soda
½ teaspoon baking powder
150 g (5 oz) dried cherries
20 g (¾ oz) flaked almonds

Preheat the slow cooker if necessary. Line the bottom of the slow cooker pot with non-stick baking paper so that it comes at least 2 cm (¾ inch) up the sides.

Whisk together the oil, almond milk, lemon rind and juice, maple syrup, vanilla bean paste, salt and ground almonds in a large bowl until well combined. Sift in the flour, bicarbonate of soda and baking powder and fold in gently. Add in three-quarters of the dried cherries and fold in gently.

Pour the batter into the slow cooker and spread it out evenly. Sprinkle the flaked almonds and remaining cherries on top.

Place a tea towel or kitchen paper underneath the slow cooker lid, cover the cooker and bake on high for 1–1½ hours until springy but firm to the touch and very lightly golden.

Remove the pot from the slow cooker and leave the cake to cool in the pot slightly. Then use the lining paper to lift the cake out of the pot and leave to cool on a wire rack. Serve warm, with some dairy-free yogurt and a dollop of cherry jam if you like, or leave to cool completely. Store in an airtight container for up to 4 days.

Seedy Banana Breakfast Loaf

(VE)

Using a loaf tin inside your slow cooker is a great hack to create a traditional, sliceable loaf. Alternatively, you can simply grease and line the bottom of the slow cooker pot with non-stick baking paper and pour in the batter, reduce the cooking time by about 30 minutes and cut the cooked 'loaf' into bars.

Makes a 900 g (2 lb) loaf
Preparation time 15 minutes
Cooking temperature high
Cooking time 1½–2 hours

3 large or 4 small very ripe bananas

60 g (2¼ oz) soya or oat yogurt

50 ml (2 fl oz) sunflower or vegetable oil

75 g (3 oz) light brown soft sugar

200 g (7 oz) plain flour

10 g (1/3 oz) baking powder

1 teaspoon ground mixed spice

1 teaspoon ground cinnamon

75 g (3 oz) mixed nuts, roughly chopped

75 g (3 oz) raisins or sultanas

25 g (1 oz) mixed seeds, such as flaxseed, pumpkin and sunflower

Preheat the slow cooker if necessary. Line the bottom and sides of a silicone or metal 900 g (2 lb) loaf tin with non-stick baking paper and grease with non-stick cooking spray or vegan butter. Ensure that the tin fits snugly inside the slow cooker pot, using some scrunched-up balls of foil to raise the tin slightly off the bottom, or to secure it if it doesn't quite reach the cooker bottom.

Mash the bananas in a large bowl, then mix in the yogurt, oil and sugar.

Sift the flour, baking powder and spices into the bowl, then fold in gently to combine until almost no dry patches remain. Gently fold in the nuts, dried fruit and seeds.

Pour the batter into the prepared loaf tin, cover with the lid and cook on high for 2 hours until the top of the loaf looks dry and a skewer inserted into the centre comes out clean, but check for doneness after 1½ hours and thereafter at frequent intervals until cooked.

Remove from the slow cooker and leave to cool in the tin for 10 minutes. Then use the lining paper to lift the loaf out of the tin and leave to cool on a wire rack.

Slice and serve still warm, leave to cool completely or toast and spread with vegan butter and jam. Store in an airtight container for up to 4 days.

For chocolate, banana & pecan bread, make the bread as above, replacing the mixed nuts with roughly chopped pecan nuts and the raisins or sultanas with vegan chocolate chips.

Banana & Cinnamon Porridge

A steaming bowl of porridge topped with vitamin-rich banana and sweet cinnamon is the perfect way to cheer up a cold winter morning.

Serves 4
Preparation time 5 minutes
Cooking temperature low
Cooking time 1–2 hours

600 ml (1 pint) boiling water
300 ml (½ pint) UHT milk
150 g (5 oz) porridge oats
2 bananas
4 tablespoons light or dark
  muscovado sugar
¼ teaspoon ground cinnamon

Preheat the slow cooker if necessary. Pour the boiling water and milk into the slow cooker pot, then stir in the oats.

Cover with the lid and cook on low for 1 hour for 'runny' porridge or 2 hours for 'thick' porridge.

Spoon into bowls, then slice the bananas and divide between the bowls. Mix together the sugar and cinnamon and sprinkle over the top.

For hot spiced muesli, follow the recipe as above, adding 175 g (6 oz) Swiss-style muesli. When cooked, stir in ¼ teaspoon ground cinnamon and top with 100 g (3½ oz) diced ready-to-eat dried apricots. Drizzle over 2 tablespoons clear honey before serving.

Overnight Turmeric Porridge

Serves 2–3
Preparation time 5 minutes
Cooking temperature low
Cooking time 4–6 hours

100 g (3½ oz) rolled oats
700 ml (1¼ pints) almond,
    soya or light coconut milk
2 teaspoons ground turmeric
    (optional)
2 tablespoons demerara sugar
1 teaspoon vanilla bean paste
pinch of salt

To serve
slices of mango
pomegranate seeds
toasted coconut flakes

Start off your day on the bright side with this sunny yellow porridge, topped with colourful mango and pomegranate seeds, or you can opt for the Spiced Plum Compote below.

Preheat the slow cooker if necessary. Put all the ingredients into the slow cooker, cover with the lid and cook on low for 4–6 hours. If your slow cooker has the function to switch over automatically to 'keep warm' once the slow cooking time is up, leave to cook overnight. Alternatively, set a separate timer to make sure the porridge doesn't overcook and burn.

Give the porridge a good stir before serving, as it will probably have a slight crust on top. Loosen with a dash of water or extra dairy-free milk if it seems dry.

Serve warm, topped with sliced mango, pomegranate seeds and toasted coconut flakes, or with Spiced Plum Compote (see below).

For spiced plum compote, to serve as an accompaniment, place 500 g (1 lb) halved and stoned plums in a saucepan with 200 ml (7 fl oz) orange juice, 2 tablespoons soft light brown sugar, 1 cinnamon stick and 2 star anise. Cook, uncovered, over a low heat for 10 minutes or until the plums are tender. Remove the cinnamon stick and star anise and serve dolloped over the porridge or dairy-free yogurt.

Brunch Poached Eggs & Haddock

For a super-healthy brunch option, opt for this low-fat, nutrient-packed combination of fish, eggs and spinach. Good for you and delicious, it's a win-win.

Serves 2
Preparation time 5 minutes
Cooking temperature high
Cooking time 1–1¼ hours

low-calorie cooking oil spray
2 eggs
1 teaspoon chopped chives
2 smoked haddock steaks,
    125 g (4 oz) each
450 ml (¾ pint) boiling water
125 g (4 oz) baby spinach
salt and pepper

Preheat the slow cooker if necessary. Spray the insides of 2 small ovenproof dishes or ramekins with a little low-calorie cooking oil spray, then break an egg into each. Sprinkle with a few chives and season to taste.

Place the egg dishes in the centre of the slow cooker pot, then arrange a fish steak on each side.

Pour the boiling water over the fish so that the water comes halfway up the sides of the dishes. Cover and cook on high for 1–1¼ hours until the eggs are done to your liking and the fish flakes easily when pressed with a small knife.

Rinse the spinach with a little water, drain and place in a microwave-proof dish. Cover and cook in a microwave on full power for 1 minute until just wilted. Divide between 2 serving plates, and top with the fish steaks. Loosen the eggs with a knife and turn out of their dishes on top of the fish. Sprinkle with chopped chives, season with salt and pepper and serve.

For brunch poached eggs with salmon, follow the recipe above, using 2 wild salmon steaks, 100 g (3½ oz) each, instead of the smoked haddock. Arrange 2 sliced tomatoes on the serving plates, top with the cooked salmon and eggs and serve.

Baked Eggs with Toast

Ham forms the cases for these little baked egg cups, with spicy chutney to add a touch of zing. Serve them with toast fingers or thick slices of the Seeded Malt Bread on page 43.

Serves 4
Preparation time 15 minutes
Cooking temperature high
Cooking time 40–50 minutes

25 g (1 oz) butter

4 thin slices of honey roast ham, 65 g (2½ oz) in total

4 teaspoons spicy tomato chutney

4 eggs

2 cherry tomatoes, halved

1 spring onion, finely sliced

salt and pepper

4 slices of buttered toast, to serve

Preheat the slow cooker if necessary. Use a little of the butter to grease 4 x 150 ml (¼ pint) ovenproof dishes (checking first that the dishes fit in your slow cooker pot). Press a slice of ham into each dish to line the base and sides, leaving a small overhang of ham above the dish. Place 1 teaspoon of chutney in the base of each dish, then break an egg on top. Add a cherry tomato half to each, sprinkle with the spring onion, season to taste, then dot with the remaining butter.

Cover the tops with greased foil and put in the slow cooker pot. Pour boiling water into the slow cooker pot to come halfway up the sides of the dishes, cover and cook on high for 40–50 minutes or until the egg whites are set and the yolks still slightly soft.

Remove the foil and gently run a round-bladed knife between the ham and the edges of the dishes. Turn out and quickly turn the baked eggs the right way up. Place each on a plate and serve with the hot buttered toast, cut into fingers.

For eggs Benedict, butter 4 dishes as above, then break an egg into each. Season to taste, sprinkle the eggs with 1 sliced spring onion and dot with 25 g (1 oz) butter. Cover and cook as above. To serve, grill 8 back bacon rashers until golden. Toast 4 halved English breakfast muffins, spread with butter, divide the bacon between the lower halves and arrange on serving plates. Top with the baked eggs and drizzle with 4 tablespoons warmed ready-made hollandaise sauce. Replace the muffin tops and serve immediately.

Eggs en Cocotte with Salmon

A special occasion calls for a special breakfast and these indulgent little ramekins of herby cream and egg accompanied by smoked salmon are just the thing.

Serves 4
Preparation time 10 minutes
Cooking temperature high
Cooking time 40–45 minutes

25 g (1 oz) butter

4 eggs

4 tablespoons double cream

2 teaspoons chopped chives

1 teaspoon chopped tarragon

200 g (7 oz) sliced smoked
    salmon

salt and pepper

4 lemon wedges, to garnish

4 slices of toast, halved
    diagonally, to serve

Preheat the slow cooker if necessary. Liberally butter the inside of 4 ramekins, each 150 ml (¼ pint), checking first that they will fit in the slow cooker pot. Break an egg into each dish. Drizzle the cream over the eggs and sprinkle over the herbs and a little salt and pepper.

Transfer the ramekins to the slow cooker pot and pour boiling water into the pot to come halfway up the sides of the ramekins. Cover with the lid (there is no need to cover the dishes with foil) and cook on high for 40–45 minutes or until the egg whites are set and the yolks still slightly soft.

Lift the dishes carefully out of the slow cooker pot with a tea towel and transfer to plates with the smoked salmon. Garnish with the lemon wedges and serve with the triangles of toast.

For spiced eggs en cocotte, break the eggs into buttered dishes and drizzle over each 1 tablespoon double cream, a few drops of Tabasco sauce and some salt and pepper. Sprinkle 3 teaspoons finely chopped coriander over the dishes and cook as above. Serve with toast and thin slices of pastrami.

Shakshuka

This take on the traditional North African and Arab dish, which includes chorizo, is a complete in-one-pan hearty brunch with the bonus of being low in calories. Serve with toast for mopping up every last bit of the tomatoey sauce.

Serves 4
Preparation time 20 minutes
Cooking temperature high
Cooking time 3¼–4¼ hours

low-calorie cooking oil spray
2 red onions, roughly chopped
75 g (3 oz) chorizo, diced
625 g (1¼ lb) tomatoes, chopped
½ teaspoon dried chilli flakes
1 tablespoon tomato purée
2 teaspoons granular sweetener
2 teaspoons paprika
1 teaspoon dried oregano
4 eggs
salt and pepper

To serve
chopped parsley
4 small slices of wholemeal bread, toasted

Preheat the slow cooker if necessary. Spray a large frying pan with a little low-calorie cooking oil spray and place over a medium heat until hot. Add the onion and chorizo and cook for 5 minutes, stirring until the onion has softened. Add the chopped tomatoes, chilli flakes, tomato purée, sweetener, paprika and oregano and season to taste.

Transfer the mixture to the slow cooker pot, cover and cook on high for 3–4 hours until the tomatoes have softened and the sauce is thick. Make 4 indents in the tomato mixture with the back of a dessertspoon, then break an egg into each one.

Cover again and cook for 15 minutes or until the eggs are set to your liking. Sprinkle with a little chopped parsley, then spoon on to plates and serve with toast.

For mixed vegetable shakshuka, follow the recipe above, omitting the chorizo and using just 1 chopped red onion. Add 1 diced red pepper, 1 large diced courgette, and 2 finely chopped garlic cloves to the frying pan with the onion and continue as above.

Tofu Shakshuka

(VE)

This is a wonderful brunch dish to serve with little effort. Accompany it with some warm flatbreads – try the homemade fennel-flavoured ones below – and you can vary the toppings; vegan yogurt works.

Serves 4
Preparation time 15 minutes, plus pressing
Cooking temperature high
Cooking time 2 hours

2 tablespoons extra virgin olive oil

1 onion, finely chopped

400 g (13 oz) can chopped tomatoes

2–3 roasted red peppers from a jar, drained and chopped

2 garlic cloves, thinly sliced

1 teaspoon ground cumin

1 teaspoon cayenne pepper

1 teaspoon sweet paprika

350 g (11½ oz) firm tofu

salt and pepper

To serve

1 avocado, peeled, stoned and sliced

small handful of coriander and flat-leaf parsley, chopped

chilli flakes

flatbreads

Preheat the slow cooker if necessary. Put 1 tablespoon of the oil, the onion, tomatoes, red peppers, garlic and spices into the slow cooker and toss until well combined. Season to taste with salt and pepper. Cover with the lid and cook on high for 2 hours until the mixture is slightly reduced. Check and adjust the seasoning.

Meanwhile, drain the tofu well, sit on a sheet of kitchen paper and top with a second piece of kitchen paper. Place a heavy bowl or chopping board on top and leave to press for 20–30 minutes, replacing the sheets of kitchen paper if they become over-saturated in liquid.

Preheat the oven to 200°C (400°F), Gas Mark 6. Cut the tofu into 2.5 cm (1 inch) cubes, toss with the remaining tablespoon of oil and season with salt and pepper. Spread out on a baking tray and roast in the oven for 25–30 minutes until golden and crispy.

Serve the shakshuka topped with the roasted tofu and sliced avocado, sprinkled with the chopped herbs and a few chilli flakes, with the warm shop-bought flatbreads or Homemade Fennel Flatbreads (see below) on the side.

For homemade fennel flatbreads, to serve as an accompaniment, put 200 g (7 oz) self-raising flour and ½ teaspoon baking powder in a large bowl. Add 1 teaspoon fennel seeds that have been roughly crushed in a pestle and mortar and a little salt and pepper. Add 2 tablespoons olive oil, then gradually mix in 6–7 tablespoons water to make a soft dough. Cut the dough into 4 pieces, then roll out each piece on a lightly floured surface until it is a rough oval shape a bit bigger than your hand. Cook on preheated griddle pan for 3–4 minutes each side until singed and puffy.

Smoky Breakfast Beans

These smoky beans are a healthier, and more flavoursome, alternative to baked beans. Try these once and you'll never go back to bought baked beans again. Pile on to hot toast and tuck in!

Serves 4
Preparation time 15 minutes
Cooking temperature low or
  high
Cooking time 3 hours (high),
  5 hours (low)

1 tablespoon olive oil

1 onion, finely sliced

3 garlic cloves, crushed

400 g (13 oz) can haricot
  beans, drained and rinsed

300 ml (½ pint) passata

1 tablespoon tomato purée

1 bay leaf

20 g (¾ oz) soft brown sugar

1 teaspoon smoked paprika

1 tablespoon apple cider
  vinegar

handful of parsley, chopped, to
  garnish

Preheat the slow cooker if necessary. Heat the oil in a frying pan, add the onion and fry over a medium-low heat for 5 minutes until soft and translucent, then stir in the garlic and fry for 3 minutes until the onion and garlic are lightly golden.

Transfer the onion mixture to the slow cooker, then add the remaining ingredients and mix together until well combined.

Cover with the lid and cook on low for 5 hours until the sauce has thickened and the beans are soft. Alternatively, cook on high for 3 hours. Serve the beans piled on to toast, sprinkled with the chopped parsley.

Baked Peppers with Chorizo

(VE)

Enjoy a brunch that has all the flavours and colours of Spain with this pepper and chorizo dish – perfect served with toast to mop up the juices.

Serves 4
Preparation time 20 minutes
Cooking temperature high
Cooking time 3–4 hours

2 large red peppers, halved
    lengthways, cored and
    deseeded
2 spring onions, thinly sliced
50 g (2 oz) chorizo, finely diced
200 g (7 oz) cherry tomatoes,
    halved
1–2 garlic cloves, finely
    chopped
small handful of basil, torn,
    plus extra to garnish
4 pinches of smoked hot
    paprika
1 tablespoon balsamic vinegar
salt and pepper

Preheat the slow cooker if necessary. Arrange the peppers, cut sides up, in a single layer in the base of the slow cooker pot. Divide the spring onions and chorizo between the peppers, then pack in the cherry tomatoes. Sprinkle with the garlic and torn basil, then add a pinch of paprika and a drizzle of balsamic vinegar to each one. Season to taste, cover and cook on high for 3–4 hours until the peppers have softened.

Transfer to a platter and sprinkle with extra basil leaves. Serve warm with hot buttered toast.

For baked pepper pizzas, follow the recipe above, omitting the chorizo and paprika. When cooked, transfer the peppers to a shallow ovenproof dish. Tear 150 g (5 oz) mozzarella into small pieces, sprinkle over the peppers, then place under a preheated hot grill for 4–5 minutes until the cheese is bubbling and golden. Garnish with extra torn basil and 4 stoned black olives.

Easy Sausage & Beans

This easy, tasty dish – featuring those old favourites, baked beans and frankfurters – is one the whole family will enjoy for breakfast. Serve with hot buttered toast fingers for dipping.

Serves 4
Preparation time 15 minutes
Cooking temperature low
Cooking time 9–10 hours or
    overnight

1 tablespoon sunflower oil

1 onion, chopped

½ teaspoon smoked paprika

2 × 410 g (13½ oz) cans baked
    beans

2 teaspoons wholegrain
    mustard

2 tablespoons Worcestershire
    sauce

6 tablespoons vegetable stock

2 tomatoes, roughly chopped

½ red pepper, cored, deseeded
    and diced

350 g (11½ oz) frankfurters,
    chilled and thickly sliced

salt and pepper

Preheat the slow cooker if necessary. Heat the oil in a frying pan, add the onion and fry, stirring, for 5 minutes or until softened and just beginning to turn golden. Stir in the paprika and cook for 1 minute, then mix in the beans, mustard, Worcestershire sauce and stock. Bring to the boil, then stir in the tomatoes, red pepper and a little salt and pepper.

Add the frankfurters to the slow cooker pot and tip the baked bean mixture over the top. Cover with the lid and cook on low for 9–10 hours or overnight. Stir well, then spoon into shallow bowls and serve with hot buttered toast fingers.

For chillied sausage & beans, fry the onion in the oil as above, then add ½ teaspoon crushed dried red chillies, ¼ teaspoon cumin seeds, roughly crushed in a pestle and mortar, and a pinch of ground cinnamon with the smoked paprika. Omit the mustard and Worcestershire sauce, then continue as above, adding the beans, stock, tomatoes, red pepper and frankfurters. Cook on low for 9–10 hours or overnight.

Sweet Potato & Goats' Cheese Frittata

A frittata is a great brunch option for entertaining. Cooked directly in the slow cooker pot this recipe is brilliantly simple and delicious. Serve warm or chill in the refrigerator to serve cold for lunch another day.

Serves 4
Preparation time 40 minutes
Cooking temperature low
Cooking time 2 hours

2 sweet potatoes, about 600 g (1¼ lb) in total, peeled and cut into bite-sized pieces
2 tablespoons olive oil, plus extra for greasing
1 onion, finely sliced
3 garlic cloves, finely sliced
6 large eggs
1 tablespoon fresh thyme leaves
50 g (2 oz) goats' cheese
salt and pepper

Put the sweet potatoes on a baking tray and drizzle with 1 tablespoon of the oil, then season well with salt and pepper and toss until well coated. Roast in a preheated oven, 200°C (400°F), Gas Mark 6, for 25–30 minutes until tender and lightly golden brown.

Meanwhile, preheat the slow cooker if necessary. Heat the remaining oil in a frying pan, add the onion and fry over a medium-low heat for 5 minutes until soft and translucent, then stir in the garlic and cook for 3 minutes until the onion and garlic are lightly golden.

Grease the slow cooker pot well with oil, then add the onion mixture and roasted sweet potatoes and mix until combined. Beat together the eggs in a large bowl. Add the thyme leaves, crumble in the goats' cheese and season well, then pour the egg mixture over the sweet potatoes.

Cover with a lid and cook on low for 2 hours until the eggs are set and a skewer inserted into the frittata comes out clean. Carefully remove the slow cooker pot from the slow cooker using oven gloves. Loosen the edge of the frittata with a knife, and turn out onto a large plate. Cut the frittata into slices and serve warm or cold.

Toffee Apple Pancakes

Kids and adults alike will love these as an indulgent brunch treat. Delicious served with thick Greek yogurt but, for an extra-special treat, top the pancakes with a scoop of vanilla ice cream.

Serves 4–6
Preparation time 10 minutes
Cooking temperature high
Cooking time 1–1½ hours

50 g (2 oz) butter

75 g (3 oz) light muscovado sugar

2 tablespoons golden syrup

4 dessert apples, cored and each cut into 8 slices

juice of 1 lemon

375 g (12 oz) pack of 6 ready-made pancakes

Greek yogurt or vanilla ice cream, to serve

Preheat the slow cooker if necessary. Heat the butter, sugar and syrup in a saucepan or in a microwave-proof bowl in the microwave until the butter has just melted. Add the apples and lemon juice to the slow cooker pot and toss together. Stir the butter mixture and pour it over the apples.

Cover with the lid and cook on high for 1–1½ hours or until the apples are tender but still holding their shape.

Heat the pancakes in a frying pan or the microwave according to the pack instructions. Fold in half and arrange on serving plates. Stir the apple mixture, then spoon it on to the pancakes. Top with scoops of vanilla ice cream.

For toffee banana pancakes, make up the recipe as above, replacing the apples with 6 small, thickly sliced bananas and adding 150 ml (¼ pint) boiling water. When ready to serve, reheat 6 pancakes, spread with 3 tablespoons chocolate and hazelnut spread, then top with the bananas and Greek yogurt.

Faster Mains (under 3½ hours)

Tear 'n' Share Marinara Bread

Seeded Malt Bread

Salmon Bourride

Chillied Sweetcorn

Caribbean Brown Stew Trout

Vegetarian Sausage &
White Bean Stew

Thai Broth with
Fish Dumplings

Smoked Haddock &
Bacon Chowder

Tomato & Red Pepper Soup

Moroccan Meatless Meatballs

Smoked Cod with Bean Mash

Braised Trout with Warm
Puy Lentils

Salmon & Asparagus Risotto

Three-fish Gratin

Mushroom Pearl Barley Risotto

Thai Fish Curry

Vegetable Biryani

Katsu Curry Sauce

Beery Cheese Fondue

Smoked Salmon Timbales

Aubergine Timbales

Mac & Cheese with Leeks &
Crispy Breadcrumb Topping

Macaroni with
Smoked Haddock

Spinach & Courgette Tian

Potato, Fennel &
Celeriac Gratin

Courgette & Broad Bean
Frittata

Aubergines with Baked Eggs

Aloo Gobi

Roasted Vegetable Terrine

Red Pepper & Chorizo Tortilla

Tear 'n' Share Marinara Bread

 (VE)

Makes 12 rolls
Preparation time 30 minutes
Cooking temperature low and
  high
Cooking time 1¾ hours

For the dough
450 g (14½ oz) strong white
  (bread) flour, plus extra for
  dusting
1 teaspoon sea salt
2 teaspoons sugar
7 g (about 2 teaspoons) fast-
  action dried yeast
1 tablespoon extra virgin olive oil
110 ml (3¾ fl oz) unsweetened
  almond milk
125 ml (4 fl oz) lukewarm water

For the marinara sauce
200 ml (7 fl oz) passata
1 tablespoon tomato purée
1 tablespoon olive oil
½ garlic clove, finely chopped
  or crushed
½ teaspoon dried oregano
  (optional)
20 g (¾ oz) Parmesan-style
  vegan cheese
salt and pepper
basil leaves, to garnish (optional)

This pull-apart pizza bread is ideal for serving with drinks and other snacks at a party. Dipping each dough ball in sauce before cooking allows you to get a beautifully crunchy, flavoursome crust on the edges and bottom of the bread. Switch up the flavours by swapping the pizza sauce for vegan pesto.

Preheat the slow cooker if necessary. Line the slow cooker pot with non-stick baking paper.

For the dough, put the dry ingredients into the bowl of a stand mixer fitted with a dough hook, add the oil and almond milk and mix briefly to combine. Gradually mix in the lukewarm water until you have a slightly sticky dough (you may not need all the water). Continue mixing on a low speed for 3–5 minutes until smooth and springy. Alternatively, mix the ingredients together with a wooden spoon in a large bowl, then turn the dough out on a lightly floured surface and knead by hand for 8–10 minutes until smooth and springy. Cover with clingfilm or a clean tea towel and leave to rest for 10–15 minutes.

Meanwhile, mix all the sauce ingredients together in a bowl. Season. Divide the dough evenly into 12 pieces. Roll each into a ball and dip into the sauce. Allow the excess sauce to drip off and put the balls into the slow cooker to form an even layer. Reserve the remaining sauce.

Cover with the lid and cook on low for 45 minutes until risen and puffy. Place a tea towel or kitchen paper underneath the slow cooker lid, re-cover the cooker and cook on high for 45 minutes. Remove the tea towel or kitchen paper, top the rolls with a few tablespoons of the reserved sauce and grate over the cheese. Position the lid slightly ajar, then cook, still on high, for a further 15 minutes.

Lift the rolls out of the slow cooker using the lining paper and serve warm, garnished with basil leaves, if you like.

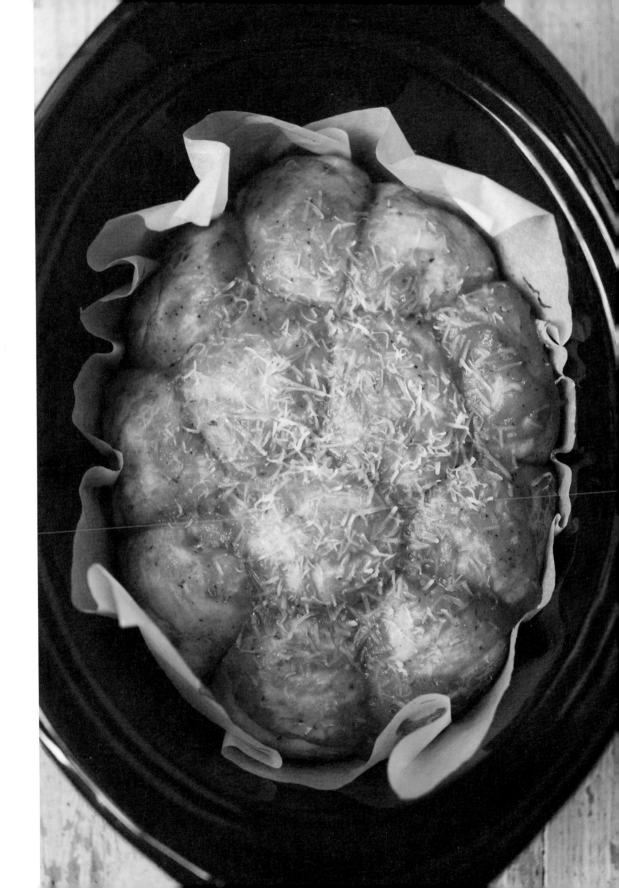

Seeded Malt Bread

Although this bread is best served fresh and still warm from the slow cooker, or toasted and slathered with salted butter, it can easily be frozen for later. Allow to cool completely, then cut into slices and freeze for up to 5 months.

Makes 1 large loaf
Preparation time 25 minutes, plus standing
Cooking temperature warm and high
Cooking time 2 hours

1 tablespoon olive oil, plus extra for greasing

200 ml (7 fl oz) lukewarm water

1 teaspoon sugar

1 teaspoon fast-action dried yeast

1 teaspoon salt

400 g (13 oz) malted bread flour, plus extra for dusting

60 g (2¼ oz) mixed seeds, such as sunflower, pumpkin, linseeds, poppy or sesame

Preheat the slow cooker if necessary. Grease a 900 g (2 lb) loaf tin with oil and set aside. Put the measured water and sugar into a large bowl and stir together until slightly dissolved. Sprinkle the yeast over the surface and whisk in, then leave to stand for 10 minutes until the surface is bubbly and frothy.

Whisk in the salt and oil, then add the flour and mix until well combined. Tip the dough out on to a lightly floured surface and knead for about 10 minutes until soft and supple.

Transfer the dough to a bowl, then place the bowl in the slow cooker. Cover with a clean tea towel, then cover with the lid. Turn the slow cooker setting to warm and leave the dough to rise for 30 minutes until doubled in size. Alternatively, if your slow cooker does not have a warm setting, place the dough in a bowl, cover with the tea towel and leave in a warm place to rise.

Remove the dough and place on a lightly floured surface. Knock back the dough, then knead in the seeds until well distributed. Transfer to the loaf tin, shaping it to fit into the corners. Place in the slow cooker, still on warm, or in a warm place, re-cover with the tea towel and leave to rise for a further 30 minutes until doubled in size again.

Carefully slash the top of the bread with a serrated knife. Re-cover with the tea towel, cover with the lid and cook on high for 2 hours until the bread is well risen and has a hard crust. Carefully remove the tin from the slow cooker using oven gloves. Transfer the loaf to a wire rack to cool.

Salmon Bourride

This simplified take on the classic French fish stew is a lovely light and low-calorie choice for a midweek meal. All it needs alongside is a bit of steamed green veg.

Serves 4
Preparation time 20 minutes
Cooking temperature low
Cooking time 3–3½ hours

low-calorie cooking oil spray
1 onion, chopped
2 garlic cloves, finely chopped
½ red pepper, cored, deseeded and very thinly sliced
½ orange pepper, cored, deseeded and very thinly sliced
400 g (13 oz) can chopped tomatoes
150 ml (¼ pint) vegetable stock
1 teaspoon granular sweetener
1 teaspoon cornflour
400 g (13 oz) can artichoke hearts, drained
4 salmon steaks, 140 g (4½ oz) each
finely grated rind of 1 lemon
½ teaspoon dried Mediterranean herbs
salt and pepper

Preheat the slow cooker if necessary. Spray a large frying pan with a little low-calorie cooking oil spray and place over a high heat until hot. Add the onion, garlic and peppers and cook for 4–5 minutes until softened. Stir in the tomatoes, stock and sweetener. Mix the cornflour to a smooth paste with a little cold water and stir into the pan. Season to taste and bring to the boil, stirring.

Transfer the mixture into the slow cooker pot, stir in the artichoke hearts, then arrange the salmon steaks in a single layer on top, pressing them down into the liquid. Sprinkle the lemon rind and herbs over the salmon and season lightly.

Cover and cook on low for 3–3½ hours until the salmon steaks are cooked and flake easily when pressed with a small knife. Spoon into shallow bowls and serve with steamed green beans.

For squid bourride, rinse 625 g (1¼ lb) prepared squid and take the tentacles out of the tubes. Slice the squid tubes and drain well. Follow the recipe above, using the sliced squid tubes instead of the salmon and cooking on low for 4–5 hours. Add the squid tentacles and continue cooking for 30 minutes until tender, then serve with the steamed green beans.

Chillied Sweetcorn

This wholesome and warming Mexican-inspired stew tastes even better the next day when the flavours have had time to meld, so any leftovers can be reheated and spooned over rice or baked potatoes.

Serves 4
Preparation time 15 minutes
Cooking temperature high
Cooking time 2–3 hours

1 tablespoon sunflower oil

1 onion, finely chopped

1 orange pepper, cored, deseeded and diced

100 g (3½ oz) frozen sweetcorn, thawed

1 garlic clove, finely chopped

large pinch of crushed dried red chillies

½ teaspoon ground cumin

1 teaspoon ground coriander

410 g (13½ oz) can mixed pulses, drained and rinsed

400 g (13 oz) can chopped tomatoes

150 ml (¼ pint) vegetable stock

2 teaspoons brown sugar

salt and pepper

To serve
8 tablespoons crème fraîche
grated Cheddar cheese

Preheat the slow cooker if necessary. Heat the oil in a large frying pan, add the onion and fry for 5 minutes, stirring, until softened. Stir in the orange pepper, sweetcorn, garlic and spices and cook for 1 minute. Add the pulses, tomatoes, stock, sugar and a little salt and pepper and bring to the boil.

Pour the mixture into the slow cooker pot, cover with the lid and cook on high for 2–3 hours or until cooked through.

Spoon into bowls and serve with the crème fraîche and cheese.

For chillied mushrooms, fry the onion as above, then add 250 g (8 oz) quartered closed-cup mushrooms instead of the pepper and sweetcorn. Fry for 2–3 minutes, then add the garlic and spices and continue as above.

Caribbean Brown Stew Trout

Serves 4
Preparation time 20 minutes
Cooking temperature high
Cooking time 1½–2 hours

4 small trout, gutted, heads
   and fins removed and well
   rinsed with cold water
1 teaspoon ground allspice
1 teaspoon paprika
1 teaspoon ground coriander
2 tablespoons olive oil
6 spring onions, thickly sliced
1 red pepper, cored, deseeded
   and thinly sliced
2 tomatoes, roughly chopped
½ Scotch bonnet or other red
   chilli, deseeded and chopped
2 sprigs of thyme
300 ml (½ pint) fish stock
salt and pepper

Brown stew is a dish popular throughout the Caribbean islands, and chilli is an essential ingredient. If you are using Scotch bonnet chillies, note that they pack a lot of heat! And do take care to wash your hands well after chopping chillies.

Preheat the slow cooker if necessary. Slash the trout on each side 2–3 times with a sharp knife. Mix the spices and a little salt and pepper on a plate, then dip each side of the trout in the spice mix. Heat the oil in a frying pan, add the trout and fry until browned on both sides but not cooked all the way through. Drain and arrange in the slow cooker pot so that they fit snugly in a single layer.

Add the remaining ingredients to the frying pan with any spices left on the plate and bring to the boil, stirring. Pour over the trout, then cover with the lid and cook on high for 1½–2 hours or until the fish breaks into flakes when pressed in the centre with a knife.

Lift the fish carefully out of the slow cooker pot using a fish slice and transfer to shallow dishes. Spoon the sauce over and serve.

For brown stew chicken, use 8 chicken thigh joints instead of the trout. Slash and dip in the spice mix as above. Fry in the olive oil until browned, then drain and transfer to the slow cooker pot. Heat the vegetables as above using 450 ml (¾ pint) chicken stock instead of fish stock, season, then cook with the chicken joints in the slow cooker on low for 8–10 hours. Thicken the sauce if liked with 4 teaspoons cornflour mixed with a little water, stir into the sauce and cook for 15 minutes more.

Vegetarian Sausage & Bean Stew

Serves 4
Preparation time 20 minutes
Cooking temperature high
Cooking time 3 hours

3 tablespoons olive oil

1 onion, chopped

2 garlic cloves, sliced

8 vegetarian sausages

2 carrots, thickly sliced

1 leek, trimmed and thickly sliced

400 g (13 oz) can chopped
   tomatoes

200 ml (7 fl oz) red wine

2 tablespoons tomato purée

2 roasted red peppers from a
   jar, thinly sliced

pinch of dried chilli flakes

½ teaspoon dried oregano

2 rosemary sprigs

2 thyme sprigs

400 g (13 oz) can haricot or
   cannellini beans, drained
   and rinsed

100 g (3½ oz) kale, stems
   removed and leaves roughly
   torn

salt and pepper

2 tablespoons chopped
   parsley, to garnish

This hearty bean and veg-filled stew uses vegetarian sausages for a twist on the French cassoulet and is full of flavour.

Heat 2 tablespoons of the oil in a large frying pan, add the onion and fry over a medium-low heat for 5 minutes until soft and translucent, then stir in the garlic and fry for 3 minutes until the onion and garlic are lightly golden. Transfer to the slow cooker.

Return the pan to the heat, add the remaining oil and the vegetarian sausages and fry for about 15 minutes until golden brown on all sides.

Transfer the sausages to the slow cooker and add the carrots, leek, chopped tomatoes, wine, tomato purée, red peppers, chilli flakes and oregano. Pour in the measured water and season well with salt and pepper, then add the rosemary and thyme. Cover with the lid and cook on high for 2 hours.

Stir in the beans, replace the lid and cook for a further 50 minutes, then add the torn kale. Replace the lid and continue to cook for 10 minutes until the kale is tender. Adjust the seasoning to taste.

Garnish with the chopped parsley and serve with creamy Sweet Potato, Cheese & Mustard Mash (see below), if you like.

For sweet potato, cheese & mustard mash, to serve as an accompaniment, place 1 kg (2 lb) peeled sweet potatoes, cut into 2.5 cm (1 inch) pieces, in a large saucepan, cover with cold water and bring to the boil. Reduce the heat, then simmer for 10–12 minutes until tender, then drain well. Return the sweet potatoes to the pan and mash until smooth. Set the pan over a low heat, push the potatoes to one side, add 25 g (1 oz) unsalted butter to the base of the pan and leave to melt. Pour 2 tablespoons milk on to butter, heat for 1–2 minutes, then add 2 tablespoons wholegrain mustard and 125 g (4 oz) grated mature Cheddar and beat into the mash. Stir in 2 tablespoons chopped chives, season to taste with salt and pepper and serve.

Thai Broth with Fish Dumplings

This spicy broth features nam pla, a staple Thai seasoning made from fermented fish. It is quite salty, so a little goes a long way. If you are feeling very hungry cook 125 g (4 oz) dried egg noodles in a saucepan of boiling water, drain and place spoonfuls in the serving bowls before ladling the soup and dumplings on top.

Serves 4
Preparation time 30 minutes
Cooking temperature high and low
Cooking time 2¼ –3¼ hours

900 ml (1½ pints) boiling fish stock
2 teaspoons Thai fish sauce (nam pla)
1 tablespoon red Thai curry paste
1 tablespoon soy sauce
1 bunch of spring onions, sliced
1 carrot, thinly sliced
2 garlic cloves, finely chopped
1 bunch of asparagus, trimmed and stems cut into 4
2 pak choi, thickly sliced, or 200 g (7 oz) Swiss chard

For the dumplings
15 g (½ oz) coriander leaves
3.5 cm (1½ inches) fresh root ginger, peeled and sliced
400 g (13 oz) cod, skinned
1 tablespoon cornflour
1 egg white

Preheat the slow cooker if necessary. Pour the boiling fish stock into the slow cooker pot, add the fish sauce, curry paste and soy sauce. Add half the spring onions, the carrots and garlic, cover with the lid and cook on high, while making dumplings.

Put the rest of the spring onions into a food processor with the coriander and ginger and chop finely. Add the cod, cornflour and egg white and process until the fish is finely chopped. Shape the mixture into 12 balls with wetted hands, then drop the dumplings into the slow cooker.

Cover with the lid and cook on low for 2–3 hours. Just before serving add the asparagus and pak choi to the broth. Replace the lid and cook for 15 minutes until just tender. Ladle into bowls.

Smoked Haddock & Bacon Chowder

This soup cooks quickly, so make sure that you chop the onion finely and cut the potatoes evenly into small cubes, about 1 cm (½ inch) in size, so that they will both cook evenly at the same time.

Serves 4
Preparation time 15 minutes
Cooking temperature high
Cooking time 2½–3½ hours

25 g (1 oz) butter

1 onion, finely chopped

300 g (10 oz) potatoes, cut into small cubes

4 rashers smoked streaky bacon, diced

750 ml (1¼ pint) boiling fish stock

1 corn cob, leaves stripped and kernels cut away from the core, or 125 g (4 oz) frozen sweetcorn, thawed

1 bay leaf

500 g (1 lb) smoked haddock, skinned

150 ml (¼ pint) double cream

salt and pepper

chopped parsley, to garnish

Preheat the slow cooker if necessary. Heat the butter in a frying pan, add the onion, potatoes and bacon and fry gently, stirring, until just beginning to colour. Add to the slow cooker pot.

Pour over the boiling stock, then add the sweetcorn, bay leaf and a little salt and pepper. Cover with the lid and cook on high for 2–3 hours or until the potatoes are tender. Add the fish and press it just beneath the surface of the stock, cutting the pieces in half if needed. Replace the lid and cook for 30 minutes until the fish breaks into flakes when pressed with a knife.

Lift the fish on to a plate with a slotted spoon and break it into flakes with a knife and fork, checking for and removing any bones. Stir the cream into the soup, then return the fish. Sprinkle with parsley and serve.

For salmon & crab chowder, fry the onion and potatoes, omitting the bacon, and continue and cook for 2–3 hours as above. Replace the smoked haddock with a 43 g (1¾ oz) can dressed brown crab meat, stirred into the potato mixture, and 500 g (1 lb) salmon fillet, cut into 4 strips and pressed below the surface of the stock. Cook for 30–40 minutes until the salmon is cooked, then continue as above.

Tomato & Red Pepper Soup

This brilliantly red soup is just the pick-me-up you need if you feel a cold coming on, as both red peppers and tomatoes are packed with health-boosting vitamin C.

Serves 4–6
Preparation time 15 minutes
Cooking temperature high
Cooking time 2½–3 hours

2 tablespoons olive oil

1 onion, chopped

1 red pepper, cored, deseeded and diced

750 g (1½ lb) tomatoes, roughly chopped

1 garlic clove, finely chopped

600 ml (1 pint) vegetable stock

1 tablespoon tomato purée

2 teaspoons caster sugar

1 tablespoon balsamic vinegar, plus extra to garnish

salt and pepper

Preheat the slow cooker if necessary. Heat the oil in a large frying pan, add the onion and fry until softened. Stir in the red pepper, tomatoes and garlic and fry for 1–2 minutes. Pour in the stock and add the tomato purée, sugar, vinegar and a little salt and pepper and bring to the boil, stirring.

Pour into the slow cooker pot, cover with the lid and cook on high for 2½–3 hours or until the vegetables are tender. Purée the soup while still in the slow cooker pot with a stick blender. Alternatively, transfer to a liquidizer and purée, in batches if necessary, until smooth, then return to the slow cooker pot and reheat on high for 15 minutes.

Taste and adjust the seasoning, if needed, then ladle the soup into bowls and garnish with a drizzle of extra vinegar or stir in spoonfuls of Spring Onion & Basil Pesto (see below).

For spring onion & basil pesto, to garnish the soup, roughly chop 4 spring onions, then finely chop with a stick blender in a jug, or in a liquidizer, with 4 sprigs of basil, 25 g (1 oz) freshly grated Parmesan, 4 tablespoons olive oil and a little pepper until a coarse paste. Spoon over the top of the soup just before serving.

Moroccan Meatless Meatballs

(VE)

Although the ingredients list may look on the long side, it results in wonderfully aromatic vegan meatballs, and you should find many of these items lurking in your store cupboard.

Serves 4
Preparation time 30 minutes
Cooking temperature high
Cooking time 2–2½ hours

1 red onion, finely chopped

3 garlic cloves

400 g (13 oz) can chopped
   tomatoes

2 tablespoons tomato purée

150 ml (¼ pint) hot stock

1 tablespoon, plus 2 teaspoons
   pomegranate molasses

1 tablespoon ras-el-hanout

1½ tablespoons ground cumin

salt and pepper

1 shallot, quartered

15 g (½ oz) fresh root ginger,
   peeled

1 red chilli

large handful of coriander, plus
   extra, chopped, to garnish

1 preserved lemon

400 g (13 oz) meat-free mince

1 slice of stale white bread,
   torn into pieces

½ tablespoon ground coriander

1 teaspoon ground cinnamon

1 tablespoon Dijon mustard

1 tablespoon olive oil (optional)

Start by making the sauce. Put the red onion, two of the garlic cloves (finely minced), chopped tomatoes, one tablespoon of the tomato purée, stock, a tablespoon of the pomegranate molasses, ras-el-hanout, a tablespoon of the ground cumin, and salt and pepper into the slow cooker. Cover with the lid and cook on high for 1 hour.

Meanwhile, put the shallot, remaining garlic, ginger, chilli and coriander, stalks and all, in a food processor. Halve the preserved lemon, scrape out the flesh with a teaspoon and discard it, finely chop the rind and add to the food processor. Blitz until you have a slightly chunky paste. Add the remaining ingredients (except the oil), including the remaining tomato purée, cumin and pomegranate molasses. Season well with salt and pepper and pulse to combine. To make sure the mixture is fully combined, squeeze it together with your hands.

Preheat the oven to 200°C (400°C), Gas Mark 6. Divide the meatball mixture into even pieces, roll each into a small golf ball-sized ball and place on a baking tray lined with non-stick baking paper. Toss the meatballs in the oil to coat and roast in the oven for 15–20 minutes until browned and caramelized. Alternatively, you can skip this step and simply poach the meatballs in the sauce.

Stir the roasted or unroasted meatballs gently into the sauce, replace the lid and cook, still on high, for a further 1–1½ hours until the sauce has reduced and thickened and the meatballs are cooked through.

Serve immediately, sprinkled with the chopped coriander, being careful when handling the meatballs as they will be quite delicate, along with the Orange & Raisin Couscous below.

For orange & raisin couscous, to serve as an accompaniment, bring 400 ml (14 fl oz) freshly orange juice and 2 tablespoons raisins to the boil in a saucepan. Put 300 g (10 oz) couscous in a heatproof bowl and pour over the orange juice mix. Cover with clingfilm and leave the couscous to steam for 5 minutes before fluffing with a fork. Stir in 1 tablespoon olive oil, a handful of chopped coriander leaves and 2 tablespoons pine nuts.

Smoked Cod with Bean Mash

Serves 4
Preparation time 15 minutes
Cooking temperature low
Cooking time 1½–2 hours

2 x 410 g (13½ oz) cans
   cannellini beans, drained
   and rinsed
bunch of spring onions, thinly
   sliced; white and green parts
   kept separate
400 ml (14 fl oz) boiling fish
   stock
1 teaspoon wholegrain mustard
grated rind and juice of 1 lemon
4 smoked cod loins, about
   625 g (1¼ lb) in total
4 tablespoons crème fraîche
small bunch of parsley,
   watercress or rocket leaves,
   roughly chopped
salt and pepper

When you can't be bothered to peel, cut and boil potatoes, bean mash is a brilliant alternative to mashed potatoes, especially if you are trying to cut carbs. Served here with brain-boosting fish, this is an all-round nutritious option.

Preheat the slow cooker if necessary. Put the beans into the slow cooker pot with the white onion slices. Mix the fish stock with the mustard, lemon rind and juice and a little salt and pepper, then pour into the pot.

Arrange the fish on top and sprinkle with a little extra pepper. Cover with the lid and cook on low for 1½–2 hours or until the fish flakes easily when pressed in the centre with a knife.

Lift out the fish with a fish slice and transfer to a plate. Pour off nearly all the cooking liquid, then mash the beans roughly. Stir in the crème fraîche, the remaining onion and the parsley, watercress or rocket. Taste and adjust the seasoning, if needed. Spoon the mash on to plates and top with the fish.

For baked salmon with basil bean mash, add the beans to the slow cooker pot with the ingredients as above, omitting the mustard. Arrange 4 x 150 g (5 oz) salmon steaks on top, season and cook as above. Mash the beans with the crème fraîche, green spring onions and a small bunch of roughly torn basil and serve with the fish as above.

Braised Trout with Warm Puy Lentils

(DF)

Many cooks consider Puy the prince of lentils for its delicate, peppery taste and because it holds its shape well when cooked. In this recipe Puy lentils provide the flavour-filled base for juicy trout steaks.

Serves 4
Preparation time 20 minutes
Cooking temperature low
Cooking time 2½–3 hours

400 g (13 oz) can Puy lentils, drained and rinsed
2 tablespoons balsamic vinegar
4 spring onions, chopped
3 tomatoes, chopped
4 thick trout steaks, 150 g (5 oz) each
finely grated rind and juice of ½ lemon
leaves from 2–3 thyme sprigs
large pinch of dried chilli flakes
150 ml (¼ pint) hot fish stock
salt and pepper
50 g (2 oz) rocket leaves, to serve

Preheat the slow cooker if necessary. Place the lentils in the slow cooker pot, then stir in the balsamic vinegar, spring onions and tomatoes. Arrange the trout steaks on top in a single layer, then sprinkle with the lemon rind and juice, thyme leaves and chilli flakes and season to taste. Pour the stock around the trout steaks, then cover and cook on low for 2½–3 hours or until the trout is cooked through and flakes easily when pressed with a small knife.

Divide the rocket leaves between 4 serving plates. Arrange the trout and lentils on top and spoon over a little of the stock. Serve immediately.

For smoked cod & spinach salad, follow the recipe above, using 100 g (3½ oz) sliced button mushrooms instead of the tomatoes, and 4 thick smoked cod loin steaks, 150 g (5 oz) each, instead of the trout. After cooking, stir 50 g (2 oz) baby spinach leaves into the lentil mixture and serve each portion topped with a poached egg.

Salmon & Asparagus Risotto

(GF)

Serves 4
Preparation time 15 minutes
Cooking temperature low
Cooking time 1¾–2 hours

25 g (1 oz) butter

1 tablespoon olive oil

1 onion, chopped

grated rind of 1 lemon

200 g (7 oz) risotto rice

150 ml (¼ pint) dry white wine

900 ml (1½ pints) fish or
    vegetable stock

4 salmon steaks, about 150 g
    (5 oz) each

1 bunch of asparagus, trimmed
    and thickly sliced

salt and pepper

chopped chives, to garnish

125 ml (4 fl oz) crème fraîche,
    to serve

Asparagus and salmon complement each other beautifully in this trouble-free risotto: there's no endless stirring, just pop it all in the slow cooker and get on with your day.

Preheat the slow cooker if necessary. Heat the butter and oil in a large frying pan, add the onion and fry for 5 minutes or until softened. Stir in the lemon rind and rice and cook for 1 minute. Mix in the wine, stock and a little salt and pepper and bring to the boil, stirring.

Pour into the slow cooker pot. Arrange the salmon steaks in a single layer on the rice, turning on their sides, if needed, so they are just below the surface of the stock. Cover with the lid and cook on low for 1¾–2 hours or until the rice is tender and the salmon flakes into opaque pieces when pressed in the centre with a knife.

When almost ready to serve, bring a saucepan of water to the boil, add the asparagus and cook for 5 minutes or until just tender. Spoon the risotto into shallow bowls and top with spoonfuls of crème fraîche, the drained asparagus and salmon steaks broken into pieces. Sprinkle with chopped chives and a little extra pepper.

For smoked fish kedgeree, add ½ teaspoon turmeric and 1 bay leaf to the fried onion instead of the lemon rind. Add 1 litre (1¾ pints) of stock, bring to the boil, then transfer to the slow cooker pot. Replace the salmon with 625 g (1¼ lb) smoked haddock, cut into 2 pieces, then cook as above. Skin and flake the fish, discard the bay leaf, then return to the pot and stir in 4 tablespoons double cream and 75 g (3 oz) just-cooked frozen peas. Spoon into bowls and top with 4 hardboiled eggs cut into wedges. Sprinkle with chopped chives and a little extra pepper.

Three-fish Gratin

Great for a low-calorie diet and packed with heart-healthy fatty acids, minerals and vitamins, this dish is so simple to make and so satisfying to eat with its crunchy breadcrumb topping.

Serves 4
Preparation time 20 minutes
Cooking temperature low
Cooking time 2–3 hours

2 tablespoons cornflour

400 ml (14 fl oz) skimmed milk

50 g (2 oz) mature Cheddar
    cheese, grated

3 tablespoons chopped parsley

1 leek, trimmed and thinly
    sliced

1 bay leaf

500 g (1 lb) mixed fish, diced
    (such as salmon, cod and
    smoked haddock)

salt and pepper

For the topping

20 g (¾ oz) fresh breadcrumbs

40 g (1½ oz) mature Cheddar
    cheese, grated

Preheat the slow cooker if necessary. Place the cornflour in a saucepan with a little of the milk and mix to a smooth paste. Stir in the rest of the milk, then add the cheese, parsley, leek and bay leaf. Season to taste and bring to the boil, stirring until thickened.

Place the fish in the slow cooker pot. Pour over the hot leek sauce, cover and cook on low for 2–3 hours until the fish is cooked through.

Transfer the fish mixture to a shallow ovenproof dish, sprinkle the breadcrumbs and cheese over the top, then place under a preheated hot grill for 4–5 minutes until golden brown. Serve with steamed peas and mangetout.

For fish pies, follow the recipe above, omitting the breadcrumb and cheese topping. Peel and cut 625 g (1¼ lb) potatoes into chunks. Cook the potatoes in a saucepan of lightly salted boiling water for 15 minutes or until tender. Drain and mash with 4 tablespoons skimmed milk, then season and stir in 40 g (1½ oz) grated mature Cheddar. Divide the cooked fish mixture between 4 individual pie dishes, spoon over the mash, rough up the top with a fork, then brush with 1 beaten egg. Cook under a preheated medium grill until golden.

Mushroom Pearl Barley Risotto

This hearty risotto is made more rustic with the use of pearl barley and is packed with earthy umami flavours from the miso.

Serves 4
Preparation time 20 minutes
Cooking temperature high
Cooking time 2½ hours

2 tablespoons olive oil, plus
    extra to serve
1 onion, finely chopped
1 leek, finely chopped
4 garlic cloves, crushed
100 g (3½ oz) chestnut
    mushrooms, chopped
100 g (3½ oz) shiitake
    mushrooms, sliced
250 g (8 oz) pearl barley
1.5 litres (2½ pints) mushroom
    or vegetable stock
1 tablespoon white miso paste
1 teaspoon fresh thyme leaves,
    plus extra to garnish
100 g (3½ oz) crème fraîche
100 g (3½ oz) vegetarian
    Italian hard cheese, finely
    grated, plus extra to serve
salt and pepper

For the garlic mushrooms
1 tablespoon olive oil
75 g (3 oz) shiitake
    mushrooms, sliced
3 garlic cloves, crushed
1 tablespoon unsalted butter

Preheat the slow cooker if necessary. Heat the oil in a large frying pan, add the onion and leek and fry over a medium-low heat for about 5 minutes until soft and the onion is translucent. Stir in the garlic and fry for a few minutes until softened. Add the mushrooms and fry for a further 3–4 minutes until just tender and beginning to turn golden.

Transfer the mushroom mixture to the slow cooker and add the pearl barley, stock, miso paste and thyme. Cover with the lid and cook on high for 2½ hours until the barley is tender and the sauce thickened. Stir through the crème fraîche and cheese and season to taste with salt and pepper.

Cook the garlic-fried mushrooms 10 minutes before the end of the risotto slow cooking time. Heat the oil in a large frying pan and add the sliced mushrooms. Fry over a medium-low heat for 3 minutes until beginning to soften. Add the crushed garlic and continue to fry for 2 minutes until the mushrooms are golden brown. Add the butter to the pan and toss to coat the mushrooms. Season with salt and pepper.

Spoon the risotto into serving bowls, then sprinkle with thyme leaves and drizzle with a little olive oil. Serve with extra grated cheese and the garlic mushrooms.

Thai Fish Curry

The secret of a great Thai curry is to use the best Thai paste you can, so be sure to choose a good-quality one for this fragrant and delicious recipe.

Serves 4
Preparation time 15 minutes
Cooking temperature low
Cooking time 2–3 hours

1 onion, quartered
15 g (½ oz) coriander leaves and stalks, plus extra to garnish
2.5 cm (1 inch) piece of fresh root ginger, peeled and sliced
1 lemongrass stalk, thickly sliced, or 1 teaspoon lemon grass paste
200 ml (7 fl oz) light coconut milk
200 ml (7 fl oz) fish stock
1 teaspoon Thai fish sauce (nam pla)
1 tablespoon Thai red curry paste
4 salmon steaks, 500 g (1 lb) in total
low-calorie cooking oil spray
400 g (13 oz) ready-prepared stir-fry vegetables
grated rind and juice of 1 lime

Preheat the slow cooker if necessary. Place the onion, coriander, ginger and lemon grass in a food processor and blitz until finely chopped.

Transfer to a medium saucepan and stir in the coconut milk, stock, fish sauce and curry paste. This mixture can be chilled until ready to use.

Arrange the salmon steaks in the base of the slow cooker pot. Bring the coconut mixture to the boil, stirring, then pour over the salmon. Cover and cook on low for 2–3 hours until the salmon flakes easily when pressed with a small knife.

Spray a large frying pan with a little low-calorie cooking oil spray and place over a high heat until hot. Add the vegetables and cook for 2–3 minutes until piping hot.

Break the salmon into large flakes and stir the lime rind and juice into the curry. Spoon into bowls and top with the vegetables and a little extra coriander.

For Thai vegetable curry, follow the recipe above to make the sauce, using 200 ml (7 fl oz) vegetable stock instead of the fish stock, and omitting the fish sauce if serving the curry to vegetarians. Place a 200 g (7 oz) can of bamboo shoots in the slow cooker pot with 175 g (6 oz) baby corn cobs, 150 g (5 oz) whole cherry tomatoes and 1 diced courgette. Pour over the sauce, cook and serve with stir-fried vegetables as above.

Vegetable Biryani

This biryani takes a little time, but the results are absolutely worth it. So save it for when you have time for some leisurely food prep and wow your family with the results.

Serves 4
Preparation time 55 minutes, plus soaking
Cooking temperature high
Cooking time 2 hours

250 g (8 oz) basmati rice

50 g (2 oz) cashew nuts

3 tablespoons coconut oil, plus extra for greasing

3 red onions, finely sliced

2 green chillies (deseeded if liked), finely chopped

2 carrots, chopped

2 potatoes, peeled and cubed

½ cauliflower, cut into small florets

1 teaspoon garam masala

1 teaspoon ground cumin

½ teaspoon ground cinnamon

5 garlic cloves, crushed

100 g (3½ oz) frozen peas

2 tablespoons tomato purée

100 g (3½ oz) passata

4 cardamom pods

3 cloves

1 teaspoon salt

2 tablespoons milk

pinch of saffron threads

1 tablespoon raisins

small handful of coriander, chopped, to garnish

Put the rice into a bowl, cover with cold water and leave to soak for 30 minutes. Meanwhile, heat a large, dry frying pan over a medium-low heat, add the cashews and toast for about 5 minutes, stirring frequently, until golden brown. Remove from the pan and leave to cool slightly, then roughly chop. Set aside.

Heat 1 tablespoon of the coconut oil in the frying pan, add the onions and fry over a medium-high heat for about 10 minutes until golden brown and caramelized. Remove with a slotted spoon and set aside.

Heat another tablespoon of the coconut oil in the frying pan, add the chillies and fry over a medium heat for 2 minutes. Add the carrots, potatoes and cauliflower and cook for 5 minutes until they begin to turn golden brown. Add the garam masala, cumin, cinnamon and garlic. Cook for a few minutes, mixing well. Stir in the peas, tomato purée and passata and heat through for 2 minutes. Set aside.

Preheat the slow cooker if necessary. Drain the rice. Bring a large saucepan of water to the boil, add the rice, cardamom, cloves and salt and cook for about 7 minutes until nearly cooked. Drain, tip into a bowl and stir through the remaining coconut oil. Set aside.

Heat the milk in a separate saucepan until warm. Remove from the heat, stir in the saffron and leave to infuse for 10 minutes.

Grease the slow cooker pot with coconut oil. Add half the vegetables and spread in an even layer, then add half the rice and spread evenly. Scatter over half the fried onions, half the raisins and half the toasted cashews. Repeat. Pour the saffron milk evenly over the surface.

Cover with the lid and cook on high for 2 hours until the rice and vegetables are tender. Sprinkle with the coriander and serve.

Katsu Curry Sauce

This spicy katsu sauce is perfect teamed with ready-made breadcrumbed seitan or tofu fillets from the supermarket. The sauce freezes really well, so make a double batch and have it on hand for an emergency dinner party.

Serves 6
Preparation time 20 minutes
Cooking temperature high
Cooking time 1 hour

2 carrots, peeled and finely chopped
2 onions, finely chopped
4 garlic cloves, finely chopped
20 g (¾ oz) fresh root ginger, peeled and finely grated
2 tablespoons plain flour
400 ml (14 fl oz) hot vegan bouillon stock
2 tablespoons garam masala
1 tablespoon curry powder
1 tablespoon maple syrup
1 tablespoon soy sauce
juice of 1 lime
1 teaspoon sea salt
1 bay leaf

To serve
breadcrumbed seitan or tofu
sesame seeds
1 lime, cut into wedges

Preheat the slow cooker if necessary. Put all the ingredients into the slow cooker, cover with the lid and cook on high for 1 hour, or on low for 3 hours.

Transfer the sauce mixture to a food processor and blitz until smooth. The sauce can be stored in an airtight container in the refrigerator for up to a week.

When ready to serve, heat the sauce up in a saucepan and serve over breadcrumbed seitan or tofu, scatter over some sesame seeds and serve along with some crisp Shaved Fennel & Radish Salad (below) and rice and lime wedges.

For shaved fennel & radish salad, to serve as an accompaniment, slice 2 fennel bulbs, about 650 g (1 lb 5 oz) in total, and 300 g (10 oz) radishes as thinly as possible on a mandolin or with a sharp knife, reserving the fennel fronds for garnish. Toss together in a large serving bowl with 2 tablespoons roughly chopped parsley. Make a dressing by whisking together 4 tablespoons lemon juice and 2 tablespoons extra virgin olive oil and season to taste with salt and pepper. Add the dressing to the salad, toss gently to mix and garnish with the reserved fennel fronds.

Beery Cheese Fondue

Throw a dinner party full of retro style with this beer-laced version of a fondue, and don't forget the traditional forfeits for dipping items accidentally dropped in the pot!

Serves 4
Preparation time 15 minutes
Cooking temperature high
Cooking time 40 minutes–
  1 hour

15 g (½ oz) butter
2 shallots or ½ small onion,
  finely chopped
1 garlic clove, finely chopped
3 teaspoons cornflour
200 ml (7 fl oz) blonde beer
  or lager
200 g (7 oz) Gruyère cheese
  (rind removed), grated
175 g (6 oz) Emmental cheese
  (rind removed), grated
grated nutmeg
salt and pepper

To serve
½ wholemeal French stick,
  cubed
2 celery sticks, cut into short
  lengths
8 small pickled onions, drained
  and halved
bunch of radishes, tops trimmed
1 red pepper, cored, deseeded
  and cubed
2 endives, leaves separated

Preheat the slow cooker if necessary. Butter the inside of the slow cooker pot, then add the shallots or onion and garlic. Put the cornflour in a small bowl and mix with a little of the beer to make a smooth paste, then blend with the remaining beer. Add to the slow cooker with both cheeses, nutmeg and some salt and pepper.

Stir together, then cover with the lid and cook on high for 40 minutes–1 hour, whisking once during cooking. Whisk again and serve with the dippers arranged on a serving plate, with long fondue or ordinary forks for dunking the dippers into the fondue.

For classic cheese fondue, omit the beer from the above ingredients and add 175 ml (6 fl oz) dry white wine and 1 tablespoon Kirsch. Cook as above and serve with bread to dip.

Smoked Salmon Timbales

These timbales are ideal as a starter at a dinner party or to kick off a big feast, like Christmas dinner. They're delicious served with thin, crispy melba toast for added crunch.

Serves 4
Preparation time 30 minutes, plus cooling and chilling
Cooking temperature low
Cooking time 3–3½ hours

200 ml (7 fl oz) full-fat crème fraîche
4 egg yolks
grated rind and juice of ½ lemon
1 large bunch basil
100 g (3½ oz) sliced smoked salmon
salt and pepper
lemon wedges, to garnish

Preheat the slow cooker if necessary. Lightly butter 4 individual metal moulds, each 150 ml (¼ pint), and base-line with circles of non-stick baking or greaseproof paper, checking first that they will fit in the slow cooker pot.

Put the crème fraîche in a bowl and gradually beat in the egg yolks. Add the lemon rind and juice and season with salt and pepper. Chop half the basil and 75 g (3 oz) of the smoked salmon, then stir both into the crème fraîche mixture. Pour the mixture into the prepared moulds. Stand the moulds in the slow cooker pot (there is no need to cover them with foil). Pour hot water around the moulds to come halfway up the sides, cover with the lid and cook on low for 3–3½ hours or until the mixture is set.

Remove the moulds carefully from the slow cooker using a tea towel and leave to cool at room temperature.

Transfer to the refrigerator and chill for at least 4 hours or overnight. Loosen the edges of the timbales with a knife dipped in hot water, then invert on to serving plates and remove the moulds. Smooth any rough areas with the side of the knife and remove the lining discs. Top with the remaining smoked salmon and basil leaves and garnish with lemon wedges.

For smoked mackerel timbales, omit the basil and smoked salmon and stir in 3 tablespoons freshly chopped chives, ½ teaspoon hot horseradish and 75 g (3 oz) skinned, flaked smoked mackerel fillets. Continue as above. Serve with salad.

Aubergine Timbales

Full of mouthwatering North African flavours of cinnamon, nutmeg, sweet dates and apricots, with a hint of garlic, these lovely little timbales make a great summer lunch al fresco.

Serves 2
Preparation time 25 minutes
Cooking temperature high
Cooking time 1½–2 hours

4 tablespoons olive oil, plus
    extra for greasing
1 large aubergine, thinly sliced
1 small onion, chopped
1 garlic clove, finely chopped
½ teaspoon ground cinnamon
¼ teaspoon grated nutmeg
25 g (1 oz) pistachio nuts,
    roughly chopped
25 g (1 oz) stoned dates,
    roughly chopped
25 g (1 oz) ready-to-eat dried
    apricots, roughly chopped
75 g (3 oz) easy-cook long
    grain rice
300 ml (½ pint) boiling
    vegetable stock
salt and pepper

Preheat the slow cooker if necessary. Lightly oil the base of 2 soufflé dishes, each 350 ml (12 fl oz), and base-line each with a circle of non-stick baking paper, checking first that they will fit in the slow cooker pot.

Heat 1 tablespoon of the oil in a large frying pan, add one-third of the aubergines and fry on both sides until softened and golden. Scoop out of the pan with a slotted spoon and transfer to a plate. Repeat with the rest of the aubergines using 2 more tablespoons of oil.

Heat the remaining 1 tablespoon of oil in the pan, add the onion and fry for 5 minutes or until softened. Stir in the garlic, spices, nuts, fruit and rice. Add a little salt and pepper and mix well.

Arrange one-third of the aubergine slices in the base of the 2 dishes, overlapping the slices. Spoon one-quarter of the rice mixture into each dish, add a second layer of aubergine slices, then divide the remaining rice equally between the dishes. Top with the remaining aubergine slices. Pour the stock into the dishes, cover with lightly oiled foil and put in the slow cooker pot.

Pour boiling water into the pot to come halfway up the sides of the dishes. Cover with the lid and cook on high for 1½–2 hours or until the rice is tender. Lift the dishes out of the slow cooker pot using a tea towel and remove the foil. Loosen the edges of the timbales with a knife, turn out on to plates and peel off the lining paper. Serve hot with a green salad or baked tomatoes.

Mac & Cheese with Crispy Topping

(V)

You can't beat a creamy and comforting mac and cheese – and this recipe is no exception. The leeks add sweetness and Emmental is a fantastic, mildly nutty Swiss cheese. The whole dish can be prepared the day before and chilled until ready to bake.

Serves 4
Preparation time 30 minutes
Cooking temperature low
Cooking time 2½ hours

50 g (2 oz) cream cheese

500 ml (17 fl oz) milk

25 g (1 oz) butter, melted

100 g (3½ oz) Cheddar cheese, grated

100 g (3½ oz) Emmental cheese, grated

50 g (2 oz) vegetarian Italian hard cheese, grated

1 tablespoon wholegrain mustard

½ teaspoon cayenne pepper

2 garlic cloves, crushed

250 g (8 oz) dried macaroni (curved elbow macaroni, if possible)

1 leek, trimmed and finely chopped

salt and pepper

1 tablespoon finely chopped chives, to garnish

For the topping

25 g (1 oz) fresh or dried panko breadcrumbs

25 g (1 oz) Emmental cheese, grated

Preheat the slow cooker if necessary. Whisk together the cream cheese and milk in a small jug until smooth. Pour into the slow cooker, then add the melted butter, cheeses, mustard, cayenne pepper and garlic and mix together. Stir in the dried pasta and chopped leek and mix until they are well coated in the sauce.

Cover with the lid and cook on low for 2½ hours until the pasta is tender and the sauce is thick and creamy. Season to taste with salt and plenty of pepper and spoon into a 16 x 22 cm (6¼ x 8½ inch) ovenproof dish.

If making this the day before, leave to cool and then place in the refrigerator overnight. When you're ready to eat, preheat the oven to 180°C (350°F), Gas Mark 4. Remove the dish from the refrigerator, cover with foil and place in the oven for 20 minutes until warmed through. Remove the foil.

Preheat the grill. Sprinkle over the breadcrumbs and grated cheese. Place under the grill for 3 minutes until golden and the cheese has melted. Serve immediately, sprinkled with the chives.

Macaroni with Smoked Haddock

Mac and cheese just went one better. This contemporary spin gives it a health boost by adding haddock, sweetcorn and spinach.

Serves 4
Preparation time 15 minutes
Cooking temperature low
Cooking time 2¼–3¼ hours

200 g (7 oz) dried macaroni

1 tablespoon olive oil

1 onion, chopped

50 g (2 oz) butter

50 g (2 oz) plain flour

450 ml (¾ pint) UHT milk

450 ml (¾ pint) fish stock

175 g (6 oz) Cheddar cheese, grated

¼ teaspoon grated nutmeg

500 g (1 lb) smoked haddock fillet, skinned and cut into 2.5 cm (1 inch) cubes

200 g (7 oz) can sweetcorn, drained

125 g (4 oz) spinach, rinsed, drained and roughly torn

salt and pepper

Preheat the slow cooker if necessary. Tip the macaroni into a bowl, cover with plenty of boiling water and leave to soak for 10 minutes while preparing the rest of the dish. Heat the oil in a saucepan, add the onion and fry gently, stirring, for 5 minutes or until softened. Add the butter and, when melted, stir in the flour. Gradually mix in the milk and bring to the boil, stirring until smooth. Stir in the stock, 125 g (4 oz) of the cheese, the nutmeg and salt and pepper and bring back to the boil, stirring.

Drain the macaroni and add to the slow cooker pot with the haddock and sweetcorn. Pour over the sauce and gently stir together. Cover with the lid and cook on low for 2–3 hours. Stir the spinach into the macaroni, replace the lid and cook, still on low, for 15 minutes.

Lift the pot out of the slow cooker using oven gloves and stir once more. Sprinkle the remaining cheese over the macaroni, then place under a preheated hot grill until the top is golden. Serve with grilled cherry tomatoes on the vine.

For Stilton macaroni with bacon, soak the macaroni as above. Make up the cheese sauce with the milk, adding vegetable stock in place of fish stock and replacing the Cheddar cheese with Stilton cheese. Omit the fish and cook as above with the sweetcorn. Stir in the spinach and 6 grilled smoked back bacon rashers, diced. Cook for 15 minutes, then finish with a little extra Stilton and brown under the grill as above.

Spinach & Courgette Tian

Based on the classic Provençal dish, this lovely combination of rice and vegetables is a great summer lunch, served with salad. So pour a glass of chilled wine and imagine you're in the south of France.

Serves 4
Preparation time 20 minutes,
Cooking temperature high
Cooking time 1½–2 hours

50 g (2 oz) easy-cook white
    long-grain rice
1 tomato, sliced
1 tablespoon olive oil
½ onion, chopped
1 garlic clove, finely chopped
1 courgette, about 175 g
    (6 oz), coarsely grated
125 g (4 oz) spinach, rinsed,
    well drained and thickly
    shredded
3 eggs
6 tablespoons milk
pinch of grated nutmeg
4 tablespoons chopped mint
salt and pepper

Preheat the slow cooker if necessary. Bring a small saucepan of water to the boil, add the rice, bring back to the boil, then simmer for 8–10 minutes or until tender.

Meanwhile, butter the inside of a soufflé dish 14 cm (5½ inches) in diameter and 9 cm (3½ inches) deep and base-line with a circle of non-stick baking paper. Arrange the tomato slices, overlapping, on top.

Heat the oil in a frying pan, add the onion and fry, stirring, for 5 minutes or until softened and just beginning to turn golden. Stir in the garlic, then add the courgette and spinach and cook for 2 minutes or until the spinach is just wilted. Beat together the eggs, milk, nutmeg and a little salt and pepper.

Drain the rice and stir into the spinach mixture with the egg mixture and mint. Mix well, then spoon into the dish. Cover loosely with buttered foil and lower into the slow cooker pot. Pour boiling water into the slow cooker pot to come halfway up the sides of the dish.

Cover and cook on high for 1½–2 hours or until the tian is set in the middle. Lift the dish out of the slow cooker using a tea towel, leave to stand for 5 minutes, then remove the foil, loosen the edge and turn out on to a plate. Cut into wedges and serve warm with salad.

For cheesy spinach & pine nut tian, omit the courgette and instead stir in 50 g (2 oz) freshly grated Parmesan cheese, a small bunch of chopped basil and 4 tablespoons toasted pine nuts.

Potato, Fennel & Celeriac Gratin

The walnut and cheese crumb in this recipe makes for a flavourful gratin that works well on its own or as a Sunday-lunch side dish.

Serves 4–6
Preparation time 1 hour
Cooking temperature high
Cooking time 2 hours

1 celeriac, about 500 g (1 lb), peeled

500 g (1 lb) floury potatoes (such as Maris Piper), peeled

1 fennel bulb, trimmed

50 g (2 oz) butter, plus extra for greasing

4 garlic cloves, finely chopped

50 g (2 oz) plain flour

1 litre (1¾ pints) milk

50 g (2 oz) Emmental cheese, grated

good grating of nutmeg

50 g (2 oz) walnuts

50 g (2 oz) fresh breadcrumbs

2 tablespoons olive oil

50 g (2 oz) vegetarian Italian hard cheese, grated

salt and pepper

Preheat the slow cooker if necessary. Slice the vegetables as thinly as possible. Grease the slow cooker pot well with butter, then layer the vegetables in the pot so they are well mixed, scattering the garlic between the layers as you go.

Melt the butter in a saucepan over a medium heat, then add the flour and stir together until it resembles a sandy-coloured paste. Cook for a few minutes until it begins to smell biscuity, then pour in a small amount of the milk, remove the pan from the heat and whisk vigorously until smooth.

Return the pan to the heat and continue to add the milk in small amounts, whisking until smooth after each addition, until all the milk has been added. Simmer for about 5 minutes until the sauce is smooth and thick. Add the Emmental and nutmeg, then season with salt and pepper. Continue to cook for a few minutes, stirring continuously, until the sauce is smooth.

Pour the sauce over the vegetables in the slow cooker, ensuring they are evenly covered. Cover with the lid and cook on high for 2 hours until the sauce is thickened and the vegetables are tender. Meanwhile, put the walnuts into a food processor and pulse until they resemble fine crumbs. Tip into a bowl, add the breadcrumbs and oil and season well. Mix together until combined, then set aside.

Preheat the oven to 180°C (350°F), Gas Mark 4. Carefully transfer the vegetables to an ovenproof dish. Sprinkle the walnut breadcrumbs and grated cheese evenly over the top, then transfer to the oven and cook for 30 minutes until golden brown and the cheese is melted and bubbling. Leave to stand for 5–10 minutes. Serve with steamed greens, or with a nut roast or whole baked cauliflower.

Courgette & Broad Bean Frittata

Serves 4
Preparation time 15 minutes
Cooking temperature high
Cooking time 1½–2 hours

40 g (1½ oz) butter

4 spring onions, sliced

1 courgette, about 200 g
   (7 oz), thinly sliced

100 g (3½ oz) podded fresh
   broad beans

6 eggs

250 ml (8 fl oz) crème fraîche

2 teaspoons chopped tarragon

2 tablespoons chopped parsley

salt and pepper

This frittata works equally well served hot or cold, so is perfect for summer picnics – weather permitting!

Preheat the slow cooker if necessary. Heat the butter, spring onions and courgette in a saucepan or in a microwave-proof bowl in the microwave until the butter has melted.

Line the slow cooker pot with non-stick baking paper, tip in the courgette and butter mixture, then add the broad beans. Fork together the eggs, crème fraîche, herbs and a little salt and pepper in a bowl, then pour into the pot. Cover with the lid and cook on high for 1½–2 hours or until set in the middle.

Lift the pot out of the slow cooker using oven gloves. Loosen the edge of the frittata with a knife, carefully turn out on to a large plate and peel off the lining paper. Cut into wedges and serve with salad.

For courgette, salmon & asparagus frittata, add 100 g (3½ oz) sliced asparagus tips to the butter, spring onions and courgette when heating and replace the broad beans with 100 g (3½ oz) chopped smoked salmon. Continue as above.

Aubergines with Baked Eggs

 (GF) (V)

Full of vegetarian protein, this is a dish you'll come back to over and over as it's delicious any time of day. It's great served with toasted pitta bread, cut into strips, for dipping into the eggs.

Serves 4
Preparation time 20 minutes
Cooking temperature high
Cooking time 2¾–3 hours 20 minutes

4 tablespoons olive oil

1 onion, chopped

2 aubergines, cubed

2 garlic cloves, finely chopped

500 g (1 lb) tomatoes, cut into large chunks

½ teaspoon smoked paprika

½ teaspoon ground cumin

½ teaspoon ground coriander

100 g (3½ oz) quinoa

300 ml (½ pint) vegetable stock

125 g (4 oz) frozen peas (optional)

4 eggs

salt and pepper

chopped mint, to garnish

Preheat the slow cooker if necessary. Heat the oil in a large frying pan, add the onion and aubergines and fry, stirring, until the aubergines are golden. Stir in the garlic, tomatoes and spices and cook for 1 minute. Mix in the quinoa and stock, add a little salt and pepper and bring to the boil.

Transfer the mixture to the slow cooker pot. Cover with the lid and cook on high for 2½–3 hours. Stir in the frozen peas, if using, and add a little boiling water if the quinoa has begun to stick around the edges of the pot. Make 4 indents with the back of a dessertspoon, then break and drop an egg into each one.

Cover and cook for 15–20 minutes or until the egg whites are set and the yolks still soft. Spoon on to plates, sprinkle the eggs with a little extra salt and pepper and garnish with chopped mint.

For aubergine ratatouille with baked eggs, omit the ground spices and quinoa and make up the recipe as above, adding 1 diced courgette and 1 cored, deseeded and diced orange pepper with the garlic, tomatoes and smoked paprika. Add 200 ml (7 fl oz) vegetable stock, season with salt and pepper and continue as above, omitting the peas. Serve sprinkled with torn basil leaves, spooned over toasted rustic-style bread.

Aloo Gobi

GF VE

This cauliflower and potato curry is the ultimate comfort food and there couldn't be an easier slow cooker recipe than this one. Simply chuck all the ingredients in and sprinkle with herbs when it's done.

Serves 4
Preparation time 15 minutes
Cooking temperature high
Cooking time 2¾ hours

2 tablespoons vegetable oil

1 large cauliflower, broken into florets

300 g (10 oz) waxy potatoes, peeled and chopped into 2–3 cm (¾–1¼ inch) chunks

1 onion, finely sliced

400 g (13 oz) can chopped tomatoes

15 g (½ oz) fresh root ginger, peeled and grated

2 garlic cloves, grated

2 teaspoons cumin seeds

½ teaspoon nigella seeds

1 tablespoon garam masala

1 teaspoon ground coriander

½ teaspoon ground turmeric

½ teaspoon chilli powder

juice of 1 lime

salt and pepper

small handful of coriander, roughly chopped, to garnish

Preheat the slow cooker if necessary. Put all the ingredients, except the lime juice, into the slow cooker and season well with salt and pepper. Cover with the lid and cook on high for 2¾ hours, stirring once halfway through if you have the opportunity, until the potato and cauliflower are easily pierced with a fork.

Season with the lime juice and serve immediately, sprinkled with the chopped coriander, along with Tamarind & Date Chutney (see below) and rice or flatbreads.

For tamarind & date chutney, to serve as an accompaniment, put 200 g (7 oz) roughly chopped stoned dates, 1 tablespoon tamarind paste, 1 teaspoon ground cumin, 1 teaspoon chilli powder, 1 tablespoon tomato ketchup, 200 ml (7 fl oz) water and a pinch of salt in a food processor or blender and process until fairly smooth. Transfer the mixture to a serving bowl, cover and chill until required. The chutney will keep for up to 3 days in the refrigerator.

Roasted Vegetable Terrine

When you want to pull out all the stops for dinner guests, this is a recipe to turn to – it's a stunner and tastes as good as it looks.

Serves 4
Preparation time 30 minutes, plus cooling
Cooking temperature high
Cooking time 2–3 hours

375 g (12 oz) courgettes, thinly sliced

1 red pepper, quartered, cored and deseeded

1 orange pepper, quartered, cored and deseeded

2 tablespoons olive oil, plus extra for oiling

1 garlic clove, finely chopped

2 eggs

150 ml (¼ pint) milk

25 g (1 oz) Parmesan cheese, grated

3 tablespoons chopped basil

salt and pepper

Preheat the slow cooker if necessary. Line a grill rack with foil. Arrange all the vegetables on the foil in a single layer, with the peppers skin side up. Drizzle with the oil and sprinkle with the garlic and salt and pepper. Cook under a preheated medium grill for 10 minutes or until softened and browned.

Transfer the courgette slices to a plate and wrap the peppers in the foil. Leave to stand for 5 minutes to loosen the skins.

Oil a 500 g (1 lb) loaf tin and line the base and 2 long sides with non-stick baking paper, checking first it will fit in the slow cooker pot. Beat together the eggs, milk, Parmesan, basil and salt and pepper in a bowl. Unwrap the peppers and peel away the skins with a knife.

Arrange one-third of the courgette slices over the base of the tin. Spoon in a little of the custard, then add the peppers and a little more custard. Repeat, ending with a layer of courgettes and custard. Cover the top with foil and put in the slow cooker pot. Pour boiling water into the pot to come halfway up the sides of the tin. Cover with the lid and cook on high for 2–3 hours or until the custard is set.

Lift the tin out of the slow cooker using a tea towel and leave to cool. Loosen the edges with a knife, turn out on to a chopping board and peel off the lining paper. Cut into slices and serve with Romesco Sauce (see below).

For romesco sauce, to accompany the terrine, fry 1 chopped onion in 1 tablespoon olive oil until softened. Mix in 2 chopped garlic cloves, 4 skinned and chopped tomatoes, ½ teaspoon paprika and 40 g (1½ oz) finely chopped almonds. Simmer for 10 minutes until thick.

Red Pepper & Chorizo Tortilla

Red peppers add colour and sweetness to this Spanish classic, cooked the slow cooker way. It's very versatile as it's delicious either hot or cold.

Serves 4
Preparation time 20 minutes
Cooking temperature high
Cooking time 2–2½ hours

1 tablespoon olive oil, plus
  extra for greasing
1 small onion, chopped
75 g (3 oz) chorizo, diced
6 eggs
150 ml (¼ pint) milk
100 g (3½ oz) roasted red
  peppers from a jar, sliced
250 g (8 oz) cooked potatoes,
  sliced
salt and pepper

Preheat the slow cooker if necessary. Lightly oil a 1.2 litre (2 pint) ovenproof soufflé dish and line the base with non-stick baking paper. Heat the oil in a small frying pan over a medium heat, add the onion and chorizo and cook for 4–5 minutes until the onion has softened.

Beat the eggs and milk together in a mixing bowl and season to taste. Add the onion and chorizo, red pepper and potatoes and toss together.

Tip the mixture into the oiled dish, cover the top with foil and put in the slow cooker pot. Pour boiling water into the slow cooker pot to come halfway up the sides of the dish, cover and cook on high for 2–2½ hours until the egg mixture has just set in the centre.

Loosen the edges of the tortilla with a round-bladed knife, turn it out on to a plate and peel off the lining paper. Cut into slices and serve hot or cold, with salad.

For cheesy bacon & rosemary tortilla, follow the recipe above, using 75 g (3 oz) diced smoked streaky bacon instead of the chorizo. Beat the eggs and milk in a bowl with the chopped leaves from 2 small rosemary sprigs, 4 tablespoons freshly grated Parmesan or Cheddar cheese and 75 g (3 oz) sliced button mushrooms. Season to taste and continue as above.

Slower Mains (over 3½ hours)

Cauliflower Cheese Soup

Mulligatawny Soup

Leek, Potato & Stilton Soup

Thai Coconut & Pumpkin Soup

Carrot & Cumin Soup

Crab Gumbo

French Onion Soup with Mustardy Emmental Croutons

Lamb & Barley Broth

Chunky Beef & Barley Broth

New Orleans Chicken Gumbo

Irish Stew

Beef Bourguignon

Beef Stew with Dumplings

Turkey & Sausage Stew

Stifado

Balsamic Beef Hotpot

Chicken & Sage Hotpot

Cidered Gammon Hotpot

Lamb Tagine with Figs & Almonds

Lentil Tagine with Pomegranate

Harissa Red Lentil & Squash Stew

Chillied Beef with Chocolate

Smoky Sweet Potato & Quorn Chilli

Spicy Bean Chilli

Gourmet Bolognese

Meat-free Mushroom Bolognese

Vegan Bolognese

Olive & Lemon Meatballs

Tandoori Chicken

Chicken & Sweet Potato Balti

Kashmiri Butter Chicken

Tofu Tikka Masala

Oriental Pork with Pak Choi

Pork with Black Bean Sauce

Tamarind Beef with Ginger Beer

Asian Glazed Ribs

Baked Seafood with Saffron

Moroccan Meatballs

Tapenade-topped Cod

Indian Spiced Cottage Pie

Chicken Cacciatore

Creamy Wild Mushroom Stroganoff

Tarragon Chicken with Mushrooms

Braised Duck with Orange Sauce

Tomato Braised Squid with Chorizo

Prune Stuffed Pork Tenderloin

Pulled Pork

Pot Roast Lamb with Za'atar Rub

Slow-cooked Lamb Shanks

Moussaka

Pot Roast Lamb with Rosemary

Turkey & Cranberry Meatloaf

Festive Nut Roast

Bacon & Leek Suet Pudding

Venison Puff Pie

Beef & Guinness Puff Pie

Mushroom Leek Thyme Pie

Root Vegetable Puff Pastry Pie

Sausage Tagliatelle

Peasant Paella

Pot-roast Pheasant with Chestnuts

Beetroot & Caraway Risotto

Fish Terrine

Duck, Pork & Apple Rillettes

Confit Tomato, Caramelized Onion & Goats' Cheese Tart

Mexican Stuffed Peppers

Cauliflower Cheese Soup

Everyone's favourite side dish takes centre stage with this deliciously creamy and cheesy cauliflower soup. Serve it with a fresh loaf of the Seeded Malt Bread on page 43 for a more substantial meal.

Serves 4
Preparation time 20 minutes
Cooking temperature low and high
Cooking time 4¼–5¼ hours

25 g (1 oz) butter

1 tablespoons olive oil

1 onion, chopped

1 small baking potato, about 150 g (5 oz), cut into small cubes

1 cauliflower, trimmed and cut into pieces, about 500 g (1 lb) prepared weight

600 ml (1 pint) vegetable stock

1 teaspoon English mustard

3 teaspoons Worcestershire sauce

100 g (4 oz) mature Cheddar cheese, grated

200 ml (7 fl oz) milk

grated nutmeg

salt and pepper

To serve
150 ml (¼ pint) double cream
ready-made croutons

Preheat the slow cooker if necessary. Heat the butter and oil in a large frying pan, add the onion and potato and fry for 5 minutes or until softened, but not coloured.

Stir in the cauliflower, stock, mustard, Worcestershire sauce, cheese and a little salt and pepper and bring to the boil. Pour into the slow cooker pot, cover with the lid and cook on low for 4–5 hours or until the vegetables are tender.

Purée the soup while still in the slow cooker pot with a stick blender. Alternatively, transfer to a liquidizer and purée, in batches if necessary, until smooth, then return to the slow cooker pot.

Stir in the milk, replace the lid and cook on high for 15 minutes until reheated. Stir and add the nutmeg to taste.

Ladle the soup into bowls, swirl cream over the top and sprinkle with a little extra nutmeg and some croutons.

For cheesy pumpkin soup, omit the cauliflower and add 500 g (1 lb) peeled and deseeded pumpkin. Dice the flesh and add to the fried onion and potato mix. Continue as above.

Mulligatawny Soup

This fragrant Indian soup is spiced with curry paste and made with creamy red lentils. Topped with the croutes for extra crunch, it's comfort in a bowl on a cold day.

Serves 4
Preparation time 15 minutes
Cooking temperature low
Cooking time 6–8 hours

1 onion, chopped

1 carrot, diced

1 dessert apple, cored and
  coarsely grated

2 garlic cloves, finely chopped

400 g (13 oz) can chopped
  tomatoes

75 g (3 oz) red lentils

50 g (2 oz) sultanas

3 teaspoons mild curry paste

1.2 litres (2 pints) boiling
  vegetable or chicken stock

salt and pepper

Croutes

50 g (2 oz) butter

2 garlic cloves, finely chopped

3 tablespoons chopped
  coriander

8–12 slices of French-style
  bread, depending on size

Preheat the slow cooker if necessary. Put the vegetables, apple, garlic, tomatoes, lentils and sultanas into the slow cooker pot.

Add the curry paste, then stir in the boiling stock and add a little salt and pepper. Cover and cook on low for 6–8 hours or until the lentils are soft and the carrots are tender.

When almost ready to serve, make the croutes. Beat together the butter, garlic and chopped coriander in a bowl. Toast the bread on both sides, then spread with the butter. Ladle the soup into shallow bowls and serve topped with the croutes.

For gingered carrot soup, put 500 g (1 lb) diced carrots and 3.5 cm (1½ inch) peeled and finely chopped fresh root ginger into the slow cooker pot with the onion, lentils and curry paste, omitting the other ingredients. Pour over 1.2 litres (2 pints) boiling vegetable stock and continue as above. Purée with a stick blender, mix in 300 ml (½ pint) milk and cook on high for 15 minutes until piping hot. Ladle into bowls and serve with swirls of natural yogurt.

Leek, Potato & Stilton Soup

This rich and filling soup is given a boost of extra taste with crispy bacon and tangy Stilton. For vegetarians, use a vegetarian blue cheese and omit the bacon.

Serves 4–6
Preparation time 25 minutes
Cooking temperature low
Cooking time 5½–6½ hours

25 g (1 oz) butter

1 tablespoon sunflower oil

500 g (1 lb) leeks, trimmed and thinly sliced; white and green parts kept separate

1 smoked back bacon rasher, diced, plus 4 grilled rashers, chopped, to garnish

375 g (12 oz) potatoes, diced

900 ml (1½ pints) chicken or vegetable stock

300 ml (½ pint) milk

150 ml (¼ pint) double cream

150 g (5 oz) mature Stilton (rind removed), diced

salt and pepper

Preheat the slow cooker if necessary. Heat the butter and oil in a large frying pan, then add the white leek slices, the diced bacon and potatoes and fry over a medium heat, stirring, until just beginning to turn golden. Pour in the stock, add a little salt and pepper and bring to the boil, stirring.

Transfer to the slow cooker pot, cover with the lid and cook on low for 5–6 hours. Stir the reserved green leek slices and milk into the slow cooker pot. Replace the lid and cook, still on low, for 30 minutes or until the leeks are tender. Roughly purée the soup in the pot with a stick blender or use a masher, if preferred.

Mix in the cream and two-thirds of the cheese and continue stirring until the cheese has melted. Taste and adjust the seasoning, if needed, then ladle the soup into bowls and sprinkle with the remaining cheese and chopped grilled bacon.

For cock-a-leekie soup, heat the butter and oil as above, then add 2 chicken thighs on the bone and fry until golden, remove them from pan and put into the slow cooker pot. Fry the leeks, bacon and potatoes as above, then mix in 1.2 litres (2 pints) chicken stock, 50 g (2 oz) pitted chopped prunes and a sprig of thyme. Season, bring to the boil, then transfer to the pot. Cover and cook on low for 8–10 hours. Take the chicken off the bone, discarding the skin, then dice the meat and return it to the pot with the green leek slices. Cook for 30 minutes, then ladle into bowls. Omit the milk, cream, Stilton and bacon garnish.

Thai Coconut & Pumpkin Soup

Make the most of autumn's bounty with this warming soup, laced with the sharp, citrussy flavour of galangal and mellow taste of coconut cream.

Serves 4–6
Preparation time 20 minutes
Cooking temperature low
Cooking time 7¼–8¼ hours

1 tablespoon sunflower oil

1 onion, chopped

4 teaspoons Thai red curry paste

1 teaspoon galangal paste

2 garlic cloves, finely chopped

1 butternut squash, about 1 kg (2 lb), peeled, deseeded and cut into 2 cm (¾ inch) chunks

250 ml (8 fl oz) carton coconut cream

750 ml (1¼ pint) vegetable stock

1 tablespoon soy sauce

small bunch of coriander

salt and pepper

Preheat the slow cooker if necessary. Heat the oil in a large frying pan, add the onion and fry until softened. Stir in the curry paste, galangal and garlic and cook for 1 minute, then mix in the squash.

Pour in the coconut cream and stock, then add the soy sauce and bring to the boil, stirring.

Pour into the slow cooker pot, cover with the lid and cook on low for 7–8 hours or until the squash is tender. (You may find that the coconut cream separates slightly but this will disappear after puréeing.)

Purée the soup while still in the slow cooker pot with a stick blender. Alternatively, transfer to a liquidizer and purée, in batches if necessary, until smooth, then return it to the slow cooker pot and reheat on high for 15 minutes.

Reserve a few sprigs of coriander for garnish, chop the rest and stir into the soup. Ladle the soup into bowls and garnish with the reserved coriander sprigs.

For pumpkin & orange soup, fry the onion in 25 g (1 oz) butter, then add the diced butternut squash with the grated rind and juice of 2 small oranges, 900 ml (1½ pints) vegetable stock and 3 whole star anise. Bring to the boil, stirring, add a little salt and pepper and continue as above. Remove the star anise before puréeing and serve with swirls of double cream.

Carrot & Cumin Soup

(V)

The flavours of carrot and cumin complement each other beautifully in this colourful soup, topped with a tangy swirl of mango chutney.

Serves 4–6
Preparation time 20 minutes
Cooking temperature low
Cooking time 7¼–8¼ hours

1 tablespoon sunflower oil

1 large onion, chopped

625 g (1¼ lb) carrots, thinly sliced

1½ teaspoons cumin seeds, roughly crushed

1 teaspoon turmeric

50 g (2 oz) long-grain rice

1.2 litres (2 pints) vegetable stock

salt and pepper

To serve

150 g (5 oz) natural yogurt

mango chutney

a few poppadums

Preheat the slow cooker if necessary. Heat the oil in a large frying pan, add the onion and fry over a medium heat, stirring, until softened. Stir in the carrots, cumin seeds and turmeric and fry for 2–3 minutes to release the cumin flavour and colour the onions.

Stir in the rice, then add the stock and a little salt and pepper and bring to the boil. Pour into the slow cooker pot, cover with the lid and cook on low for 7–8 hours or until the carrots are tender.

Purée the soup while still in the slow cooker pot with a stick blender. Alternatively, transfer to a liquidizer and purée, in batches if necessary, until smooth, then return to the slow cooker pot and reheat on high for 15 minutes.

Taste and adjust the seasoning, if needed, then ladle the soup into bowls. Top with spoonfuls of yogurt and a little mango chutney and serve with poppadums.

For spiced parsnip soup, fry the onion as above, replacing the carrots with 625 g (1¼ lb) halved and thinly sliced parsnips and adding 1 teaspoon turmeric, 1 teaspoon ground cumin, 1 teaspoon ground coriander and 3.5 cm (1½ inch) peeled and finely chopped fresh root ginger. Continue as above.

Crab Gumbo

Official cuisine of the state of Louisiana, gumbo is a spicy soup or stew made with a variety of meat and seafood. This super-easy version pares things back with delicate crab meat.

Serves 4
Preparation time 15 minutes
Cooking temperature high
Cooking time 3¼ hours–4½ hours

1 tablespoon sunflower oil
1 onion, finely chopped
1 garlic clove, chopped
2 celery sticks, sliced
1 carrot, cut into small dice
400 g (13 oz) can chopped tomatoes
600 ml (1 pint) fish stock
50 g (2 oz) easy-cook long-grain rice
1 bay leaf
2 sprigs of thyme
¼ teaspoon crushed dried red chillies
75 g (3 oz) okra, sliced
43 g (1¾ oz) can dressed brown crab meat
salt and pepper
170 g (5¾ oz) can white crab meat, to serve (optional)

Preheat the slow cooker if necessary. Heat the oil in a large frying pan, add the onion and fry for 5 minutes or until softened.

Stir in the garlic, celery and carrot, then mix in the tomatoes, stock, rice, herbs and chillies. Add a little salt and pepper and bring to the boil.

Pour into the slow cooker pot, cover with the lid and cook on high for 3–4 hours or until the vegetables and rice are tender.

Stir the soup, then add the okra and dressed brown crab meat. Replace the lid and cook, still on high, for 20–30 minutes. Ladle the soup into bowls, top with the flaked white crab meat, if liked, and serve with warm crusty bread.

For mixed vegetable gumbo, make up the soup as above, omitting the cans of brown and white crab meat. Garnish with croutons made by frying 2 slices of bread, cut into cubes, in 25 g (1 oz) butter, 3 tablespoons olive oil and ¼ teaspoon crushed dried red chillies until golden.

French Onion Soup & Cheesy Croutons

A French classic. The best versions are cooked for a long time over a low heat, so the onions become very soft and the broth is full of flavour. This recipe is worth the long cook time – you will never rush a French onion soup again!

Serves 4
Preparation time 20 minutes
Cooking temperature low
Cooking time 12 hours

100 g (3½ oz) butter

2 tablespoons olive oil

875 g (1¾ lb) white onions, sliced

1 teaspoon sea salt

1.5 litres (2½ pints) vegetable stock

150 ml (¼ pint) white wine

2 tablespoons balsamic vinegar

3 thyme sprigs

pepper

chopped thyme, to garnish

For the croutons

1 French stick, cut into 8 x 1 cm (½ inch) slices

olive oil, for drizzling

25 g (1 oz) Dijon mustard

100 g (3½ oz) Emmental cheese, grated

Preheat the slow cooker if necessary. Put the butter and oil into the slow cooker, turn on to low and leave until the butter begins to melt, then add the onions and salt and mix together until the onions are well coated. Cover with the lid and cook for 4 hours until the onions are soft, tender and caramelized, stirring occasionally to ensure the onions are not sticking to the pot.

Pour in the stock, wine, balsamic vinegar and thyme, replace the lid and cook, still on low, for a further 6 hours until the soup is reduced and full of flavour. Season to taste with salt and pepper.

When ready to serve, preheat the grill. Drizzle the bread slices with a little oil, then cook under the grill until lightly toasted on each side. Spread each slice with a thin layer of the mustard.

Ladle the soup into 4 heatproof bowls, then top each one with 2 slices of the toasted bread and sprinkle liberally with the grated cheese. Place the bowls under the grill and cook for 3–5 minutes until the cheese has melted and is bubbly and golden. Serve immediately, sprinkled with chopped thyme.

Lamb & Barley Broth

The flavours of carrot and cumin complement each other beautifully in this colourful soup, topped with a tangy swirl of mango chutney.

Serves 4
Preparation time 15 minutes
Cooking temperature low
Cooking time 8–10 hours

25 g (1 oz) butter

1 tablespoon sunflower oil

1 lamb rump chop or 125 g
   (4 oz) lamb fillet, diced

1 onion, chopped

1 small leek, trimmed and
   chopped

500 g (1 lb) mixed parsnip,
   swede, turnip and carrot, cut
   into small dice

50 g (2 oz) pearl barley

1.2 litres (2 pints) lamb or
   chicken stock

¼ teaspoon ground allspice

2–3 rosemary sprigs

salt and pepper

chopped parsley or chives, to
   garnish

Preheat the slow cooker if necessary. Heat the butter and oil in a large frying pan over a high heat, add the lamb, onion and leek and cook, stirring, for 5 minutes until the lamb is lightly browned.

Stir in the root vegetables and barley, then add the stock, allspice and rosemary. Season to taste and bring to the boil, stirring.

Pour into the slow cooker pot, cover and cook on low for 8–10 hours or until the barley is tender. Stir well, taste and adjust the seasoning, if necessary, then ladle the soup into bowls. Garnish with chopped herbs and serve.

For Hungarian chorba, follow the recipe above, adding 1 teaspoon smoked paprika, 50 g (2 oz) long-grain rice and a few sprigs of dill instead of the pearl barley. Stir in 1.2 litres (2 pints) lamb stock, 2 tablespoons red wine vinegar and 1 tablespoon light muscovado sugar. Season to taste, bring to the boil and continue as above. Garnish with chopped dill and serve with rye bread.

Chunky Beef & Barley Broth

Thick with nourishing pearl barley and lentils and packed with health-giving ingredients, this hearty soup is a complete meal in a bowl.

Serves 4
Preparation time 15 minutes
Cooking temperature high
Cooking time 5¼–6¼ hours

300 g (10 oz) lean stewing beef, diced
250 g (8 oz) swede, finely diced
250 g (8 oz) carrot, finely diced
1 onion, finely chopped
50 g (2 oz) pearl barley
50 g (2 oz) dried red lentils
900 ml (1½ pints) hot beef stock
1 teaspoon dried mixed herbs
1 teaspoon mustard powder
1 tablespoon Worcestershire sauce
125 g (4 oz) green cabbage, thinly shredded
salt and pepper

Preheat the slow cooker if necessary. Heat the butter and oil in a large frying pan over a high heat, add the lamb, onion and leek and cook, stirring, for 5 minutes until the lamb is lightly browned.

Stir in the root vegetables and barley, then add the stock, allspice and rosemary. Season to taste and bring to the boil, stirring.

Pour into the slow cooker pot, cover and cook on low for 8–10 hours or until the barley is tender. Stir well, taste and adjust the seasoning, if necessary, then ladle the soup into bowls. Garnish with chopped herbs and serve.

For chicken & barley broth, follow the recipe above, using 300 g (10 oz) boneless, skinless diced chicken thighs and 1 sliced leek instead of the beef and onion. Use 900 ml (1½ pints) chicken stock instead of the beef stock, and 50 g (2 oz) diced pitted prunes instead of the Worcestershire sauce. Cook as above, adding the cabbage for the last 15 minutes.

New Orleans Chicken Gumbo

All the authentic flavours of New Orleans are here: chicken, sausage, colourful veg, rice and a kick of cayenne. Ladle out a bowlful and enjoy!

Serves 4
Preparation time 20 minutes
Cooking temperature low and
high
Cooking time 8¼–10¼ hours

2 tablespoons olive oil

500 g (1 lb) boneless, skinless
chicken thighs, cubed

75 g (3 oz) ready-diced chorizo

75 g (3 oz) smoked streaky
bacon, diced

1 onion, sliced

2 garlic cloves, chopped

2 tablespoons plain flour

600 ml (1 pint) chicken stock

2 bay leaves

2 sprigs of thyme

salt

¼–½ teaspoon cayenne
pepper, to taste

3 celery sticks, sliced

½ each of 3 different coloured
peppers, cored, deseeded
and sliced

125 g (4 oz) okra, thickly sliced
(optional)

chopped parsley, to garnish

Preheat the slow cooker if necessary. Heat the oil in a large frying pan, add the chicken a few pieces at time until all the pieces are in the pan, then add the chorizo and bacon and fry, stirring, until the chicken is golden. Lift out of the pan with a slotted spoon and transfer to the slow cooker.

Add the onion to the frying pan and fry until softened. Mix in the garlic, then stir in the flour. Gradually mix in the stock, add the herbs and a little salt and cayenne to taste. Bring to the boil, stirring.

Mix the celery and different coloured peppers into the chicken, then pour over the hot onion mixture. Cover with the lid and cook on low for 8–10 hours or until the chicken is cooked through.

When almost ready to serve, stir the okra into the chicken gumbo, if using. Replace the lid and cook on high for 15 minutes or until the okra has just softened. Stir once more, then sprinkle with chopped parsley. Ladle into shallow rice-lined bowls and serve with a soup spoon and fork.

Irish Stew

Cooked slowly, this stew makes the best of cheaper cuts of lamb. Serve it with plenty of crusty bread to soak up the gravy.

Serves 4
Preparation time 20 minutes
Cooking temperature high
Cooking time 6–7 hours

2 tablespoons sunflower oil

1 kg (2 lb) stewing lamb

1 onion, roughly chopped

3 carrots, sliced

250 g (8 oz) swede, diced

250 g (8 oz) parsnips, diced

2 tablespoons plain flour

400 g (13 oz) potatoes, cut into chunks no bigger than 4 cm (1½ inch) square

800 ml (1 pint 7 fl oz) lamb or chicken stock

3 sprigs of rosemary

salt and pepper

4 tablespoons mixed chopped chives and rosemary, to garnish

Preheat the slow cooker if necessary. Heat the oil in a large frying pan, add the lamb and fry until browned on both sides. Scoop out of the pan with a slotted spoon and transfer to a plate.

Add the onion to the pan and fry for 5 minutes or until softened. Add the carrots, swede and parsnips and cook for 1–2 minutes, then stir in the flour. Add the potatoes, stock, rosemary and plenty of salt and pepper and bring to the boil, stirring.

Pour into the slow cooker pot, add the lamb and press below the surface of the liquid. Cover with the lid and cook on high for 6–7 hours or until the lamb is falling off the bones and the potatoes are tender.

Spoon into shallow bowls, removing the lamb bones if liked, and sprinkle with the chopped chives and rosemary. Serve with a spoon and fork and crusty bread.

For lamb stew with dumplings, make up the stew as above. About 35–50 minutes before the end of cooking, mix 150 g (5 oz) self-raising flour, 75 g (3 oz) vegetable suet, 2 teaspoons chopped rosemary leaves and a little salt and pepper in a bowl. Stir in 5–7 tablespoons water to make a soft but not sticky dough. Shape into 12 balls, add to the slow cooker pot, cover and cook on high for 30–45 minutes until well risen.

Beef Bourguignon

Tender, fall-apart beef simmered in a rich red wine gravy – this low-fat take on the much-loved French classic packs a lot of flavour.

Serves 4
Preparation time 20 minutes
Cooking temperature low
Cooking time 10–11 hours

low-calorie cooking oil spray
625 g (1¼ lb) stewing beef,
    trimmed of fat and cubed
100 g (3½ oz) bacon, diced
300 g (10 oz) small shallots,
    peeled
3 garlic cloves, finely chopped
1 tablespoon plain flour
150 ml (¼ pint) red wine
300 ml (½ pint) beef stock
1 tablespoon tomato purée
small bunch of mixed herbs or
    a dried bouquet garni
salt and pepper
chopped parsley, to garnish

Preheat the slow cooker if necessary. Spray a large frying pan with a little low-calorie cooking oil spray and place over a high heat until hot. Add the beef, a few pieces at a time until all the beef is in the pan, and cook for 5 minutes, stirring, until browned.

Use a slotted spoon to transfer the beef to the slow cooker pot. Add the bacon and shallots to the frying pan and cook over a medium heat for 2–3 minutes until the bacon is just beginning to brown. Stir in the garlic and flour, then add the wine, stock, tomato purée and herbs. Season to taste and bring to the boil, stirring.

Pour the sauce over the beef, cover and cook on low for 10–11 hours until the beef is tender. Stir, garnish with chopped parsley and serve with rice.

For beef goulash, follow the recipe above, adding 2 teaspoons mild paprika, 1 teaspoon caraway seeds, ¼ teaspoon ground cinnamon and ¼ teaspoon ground allspice instead of the herbs.

Beef Stew with Dumplings

Cooked low and slow, this stew, with its light and fluffy horseradish-spiked dumplings, is just the thing you'll want on the coldest of wintery nights.

Serves 4
Preparation time 35 minutes
Cooking temperature low and
  high
Cooking time 8–10½ hours

2 tablespoons olive oil

750 g (1½ lb) braising beef,
  trimmed of fat and cubed

1 large onion, chopped

2–3 garlic cloves, chopped

2 tablespoons plain flour

300 ml (½ pint) Burgundy red
  wine

300 ml (½ pint) beef stock

1 tablespoon tomato purée

2 bay leaves

150 g (5 oz) baby carrots,
  larger ones halved

250 g (8 oz) leeks, trimmed
  and thinly sliced

salt and pepper

For the horseradish dumplings

150 g (5 oz) self-raising flour,
  plus extra for dusting

75 g (3 oz) shredded suet

2 teaspoons creamed
  horseradish

3 tablespoons snipped chives

5–7 tablespoons water

Preheat the slow cooker if necessary. Heat the oil in a frying pan and add the beef a few pieces at a time until all the meat is in the pan. Fry over a high heat until just beginning to brown, then add the onion and fry, stirring, for 5 minutes.

Stir in the garlic and flour, then gradually mix in the wine and stock. Add the tomato purée and bay leaves and season with salt and pepper. Bring to the boil, then transfer the mixture to the slow cooker pot. Cover with the lid and cook on low for 7–9 hours.

Stir the stew, then add the carrots, replace the lid and cook on high for 30–45 minutes.

Meanwhile, make the dumplings. Mix the flour, suet, horseradish, chives and salt and pepper together in a bowl. Stir in enough of the measured water to make a soft but not sticky dough. With floured hands, shape into 8 balls.

Stir the leeks into the stew, then add the dumplings, replace the lid and cook, still on high, for another 30–45 minutes or until the dumplings are light and fluffy. Spoon into shallow dishes and serve, remembering to remove the bay leaves.

For Guinness beef stew with mustard dumplings, make up the stew as above, replacing the red wine with 300 ml (½ pint) Guinness or stout. Top with dumplings made with 3 teaspoons wholegrain mustard instead of the creamed horseradish and chives.

Turkey & Sausage Stew

(DF)

This is sure to be a cold weather family favourite – the cranberries give the stew a tangy zing and the dumplings are lovely atop any stew or soup, not just with this recipe.

Serves 4
Preparation time 30 minutes
Cooking temperature high
Cooking time 5½–6¾ hours

1 turkey drumstick, about
   700 g (1 lb 6 oz)
2 tablespoons sunflower oil
4 smoked streaky bacon
   rashers, diced
3 large pork and herb
   sausages, about 200 g (7 oz)
   in total, each cut into 4 pieces
1 onion, sliced
1 leek, trimmed and sliced; white
   and green parts kept separate
2 tablespoons plain flour
600 ml (1 pint) chicken stock
small bunch of mixed herbs
300 g (10 oz) baby carrots,
   halved if large
2 celery sticks, sliced
65 g (2½ oz) fresh cranberries
salt and pepper

For the parsley dumplings
150 g (5 oz) self-raising flour
75 g (3 oz) shredded suet
4 tablespoons chopped parsley
5–7 tablespoons water

Preheat the slow cooker if necessary. If the turkey drumstick does not fit into the slow cooker pot sever the knuckle end with a large heavy knife, hitting it with a rolling pin.

Heat the oil in a large frying pan, add the drumstick, bacon and sausage pieces and fry, turning until browned all over. Transfer to the slow cooker pot. Add the onion and white leeks slices to the pan and fry until softened. Stir in the flour, then mix in the stock. Add the herbs, salt and pepper and bring to the boil.

Add the carrots, celery and cranberries to the pot and pour over the hot onion mixture. Cover with the lid and cook on high for 5–6 hours or until the turkey is almost falling off the bone. Lift the turkey out of the slow cooker pot. Remove and discard the skin, then cut the meat into pieces, discarding the bones and tendons. Return meat to the pot with the reserved green leek slices.

Make the dumplings. Mix the flour, suet, parsley and salt and pepper in a bowl. Stir in enough water to make a soft dough. Knead, then shape into 12 small balls. Arrange over the turkey, replace the lid and cook, still on high, for 30–45 minutes or until the dumplings are cooked through. Spoon into shallow bowls to serve.

For turkey & cranberry puff pie, make the stew as above. Roll out 500 g (1 lb) puff pastry, trim to an oval a little larger than the top of the slow cooker pot and put on an oiled baking sheet. Brush the top with beaten egg, then bake in a preheated oven at 200°C (400°F), Gas Mark 6 for about 25 minutes until golden. Spoon the stew on to plates and top with wedges of the pastry.

Stifado

This popular Greek dish combines melt-in-the-mouth beef with an intense wine and tomato sauce. It's perfect served with crusty French bread and herbed-flecked butter.

Serves 4

Preparation time 25 minutes, plus overnight marinating

Cooking temperature high and low

Cooking time 9½–10½ hours

200 ml (7 fl oz) red wine

1 tablespoon tomato purée

2 tablespoons olive oil

2–3 sprigs of thyme or bay leaves

4 cloves

¼ teaspoon ground allspice

300 g (10 oz) shallots, halved if large

2 garlic cloves, finely chopped

750 g (1½ lb) stewing beef, cut into large chunks and any fat discarded

4 teaspoons cornflour

150 ml (¼ pint) cold water

½ beef stock cube

salt and pepper

Mix the wine, tomato purée and oil in a shallow non-metallic dish. Add the herbs, spices and a little salt and pepper and mix together. Mix in the shallots and garlic, then add the beef and toss in the marinade. Cover with clingfilm and marinate in the refrigerator overnight.

Preheat the slow cooker if necessary. Put the cornflour into a saucepan, mix in a little of the water to make a smooth paste, then mix in the remaining water. Drain the marinade from the beef into the pan and crumble in the stock cube. Bring to the boil, stirring.

Tip the beef, shallots and flavourings into the slow cooker pot and pour over the hot stock. Cover with the lid and cook on high for 30 minutes. Reduce the heat and cook on low for 9½–10½ hours until the meat is cooked through and tender. Spoon into bowls and serve.

For lamb stifado, mix together 200 ml (7 fl oz) white wine, 1 tablespoon tomato purée, 2 tablespoons olive oil, 2 bay leaves, 2 teaspoons roughly crushed coriander seeds and ½ sliced lemon, add the shallots and garlic and stir in 750 g (1½ lb) diced lamb shoulder or leg. Marinate overnight, then continue as above.

Balsamic Beef Hotpot

Comfort food doesn't get much better than a hotpot. Serve this low-fat version with plenty of steamed green veg for a delicious midweek supper.

Serves 4
Preparation time 30 minutes
Cooking temperature high
Cooking time 7–8 hours

low-calorie cooking oil spray
600 g (1 lb) lean stewing beef, trimmed of fat and cubed
1 onion, chopped
250 g (8 oz) swede, cut into 2 cm (¾ inch) cubes
300 g (10 oz) carrots, sliced
150 g (5 oz) mushrooms, sliced
2 teaspoons plain flour
450 ml (¾ pint) beef stock
2 tablespoons balsamic vinegar
1 teaspoon mustard powder
500 g (1 lb) potatoes, sliced
salt and pepper
1 tablespoon chopped parsley, to garnish

Preheat the slow cooker if necessary. Spray a large frying pan with a little low-calorie cooking oil spray and place over a high heat until hot. Add the beef a few pieces at a time until all the beef is in the pan and cook for 5 minutes, stirring, until browned. Use a slotted spoon to transfer the beef to the slow cooker pot.

Add a little more low-calorie cooking oil spray to the pan, add the onion and cook for 4–5 minutes until beginning to brown. Add the swede, carrots and mushrooms and cook for 2 minutes. Add the flour and stir well.

Stir in the stock, vinegar and mustard, season to taste and bring to the boil. Pour over the beef in the slow cooker pot. Arrange the potato slices on top, slightly overlapping. Season lightly, then press the potatoes into the stock. Cover and cook on high for 7–8 hours until the potatoes and beef are tender.

Lift the pot out of the slow cooker using oven gloves. Spray the potatoes with a little extra low-calorie cooking oil spray, then place under a preheated hot grill until the potatoes are golden. Sprinkle with the parsley and serve with some steamed green vegetables.

Chicken & Sage Hotpot

With its crispy, golden potato topping, this dish is the perfect fuss-free family meal. Serve it with steamed green beans or broccoli.

Serves 4
Preparation time 30 minutes
Cooking temperature high
Cooking time 4–5 hours

1 tablespoon sunflower oil

6 boneless, skinless chicken thighs, about 550 g (1 lb 2 oz), each cut into 3 pieces

1 onion, sliced

4 smoked streaky bacon rashers, diced

2 tablespoons plain flour

600 ml (1 pint) chicken stock or a mix of stock and dry cider

2–3 sprigs of sage

125 g (4 oz) black pudding, diced (optional)

200 g (7 oz) carrots, diced

200 g (7 oz) swede, diced

625 g (1¼ lb) potatoes, thinly sliced

25 g (1 oz) butter

salt and pepper

Preheat the slow cooker if necessary. Heat the oil in a large frying pan, add the chicken a few pieces at a time until all the meat is in the pan, then add the onion and bacon and fry, stirring, until the chicken is golden.

Stir in the flour, then gradually mix in the stock. Add the sage sprigs and a little salt and pepper and bring to the boil, stirring. Add the black pudding, if using, carrots and swede to the slow cooker pot.

Pour over the hot chicken mixture, then arrange the potatoes overlapping on the top and press below the surface of the liquid. Sprinkle with a little extra salt and pepper, then cover with the lid and cook on high for 4–5 hours or until the potatoes are tender and the chicken is cooked through.

Lift the pot out of the slow cooker using oven gloves, dot the potatoes with butter and brown under a hot grill. Spoon into shallow dishes to serve.

For mustardy beef hotpot, replace the chicken with 750 g (1½ lb) trimmed and diced stewing beef. Fry the beef in the oil and transfer to the slow cooker pot, then fry the onion, omitting the bacon. Stir in the flour, then mix in 600 ml (1 pint) beef stock, 2 teaspoons English mustard, 1 tablespoon Worcestershire sauce, 1 tablespoon tomato purée and salt and pepper and bring to the boil. Omit the black pudding and continue as above.

Cidered Gammon Hotpot

Serves 4
Preparation time 25 minutes
Cooking temperature high
Cooking time 6–7 hours

500 g (1 lb) unsmoked
   gammon joint, trimmed of fat
625 g (1¼ lb) baking potatoes,
   cut into 2 cm (¾ inch)
   chunks
200 g (7 oz) small shallots,
   peeled
3 carrots, thickly sliced
2 celery sticks, thickly sliced
1 large leek, trimmed and
   thickly sliced
2 bay leaves
200 ml (7 fl oz) dry cider
200 ml (7 fl oz) hot chicken
   stock
¼ teaspoon cloves
1 teaspoon mustard powder
pepper
3 tablespoons chopped chives,
   to garnish

Pork and apple is a classic pairing and the fruity cider in this hotpot really lifts the taste of the gammon. If you are cooking for children, you could use a mixture of apple juice and water instead.

Preheat the slow cooker if necessary. Rinse the gammon joint with cold water and place in the slow cooker pot with the potatoes. Arrange the shallots, carrots, celery and leek slices around the gammon, then tuck in the bay leaves.

Pour the cider and stock into a saucepan, add the cloves and mustard powder, then season with pepper (gammon joints can be salty so don't be tempted to add salt). Bring to the boil, then pour around the gammon. Cover and cook on high for 6–7 hours until the gammon is cooked through.

Cut the gammon into pieces and serve in shallow bowls with the vegetables and stock, garnished with chopped chives.

For gammon in cola, follow the recipe above, using 450 ml (¾ pint) diet cola instead of the cider and stock and omitting the potatoes.

Lamb Tagine with Figs & Almonds

Serves 4
Preparation time 15 minutes
Cooking temperature low
Cooking time 8–10 hours

1 tablespoon olive oil

750 g (1½ lb) lamb fillet, diced, or ready-diced lamb

1 onion, sliced

2 garlic cloves, finely chopped

2.5 cm (1 inch) piece of fresh root ginger, peeled and finely chopped

2 tablespoons plain flour

600 ml (1 pint) lamb stock

1 teaspoon ground cinnamon

2 large pinches of saffron threads

75 g (3 oz) dried figs, stalks trimmed and diced

40 g (1½ oz) toasted flaked almonds

salt and pepper

Tagine is a North African casserole named after the earthenware pot it is traditionally cooked in. This slow cooker version gives you all the authentic flavours of North Africa the easy way.

Preheat the slow cooker if necessary. Heat the oil in a frying pan, add the lamb a few pieces at a time until all the meat is in the pan, then fry over a high heat, stirring until browned. Remove from the pan with a slotted spoon and transfer to the slow cooker pot.

Add the onion and fry, stirring, for 5 minutes or until softened and just beginning to turn golden. Stir in the garlic and ginger, then mix in the flour. Gradually stir in the stock. Add the spices, figs and a little salt and pepper and bring to the boil, stirring.

Spoon into the slow cooker pot, cover and cook on low for 8–10 hours or until the lamb is tender. Stir, then sprinkle with the toasted flaked almonds. Serve with Lemon & Chickpea Couscous (see below).

For lemon & chickpea couscous, to serve as an accompaniment, put 200 g (7 oz) couscous into a bowl, add the grated rind and juice of 1 lemon, 2 tablespoons olive oil, a 410 g (13½ oz) can chickpeas, drained and rinsed, and some salt and pepper. Pour over 450 ml (¾ pint) boiling water, then cover the bowl with a plate and leave to stand for 5 minutes. Remove the plate, add 4 tablespoons chopped parsley or coriander and fluff up with a fork.

Lentil Tagine with Pomegranate

Serves 4
Preparation time 15 minutes
Cooking temperature high
Cooking time 4–5 hours

1 tablespoon olive oil

1 onion, chopped

5 cm (2 inch) piece of fresh
    root ginger, peeled and finely
    chopped

3 garlic cloves, finely chopped

2 teaspoons cumin seeds,
    crushed

1 teaspoon coriander seeds,
    crushed

200 g (7 oz) dried Puy lentils

2 celery sticks, sliced

250 g (8 oz) cherry tomatoes,
    halved

450 ml (¾ pint) hot vegetable
    stock

juice of 1 lemon

15 g (½ oz) flat-leaf parsley,
    roughly chopped

15 g (½ oz) mint, roughly
    chopped

To serve
125 ml (4 fl oz) fat-free yogurt
seeds from ½ pomegranate

There is a sweetness and spiciness to this vegetarian tagine, packed with fibre-rich lentils. Served with a dollop of yogurt and some juicy pomegranate seeds, it's a brilliant low-fat, health-packed meal.

Preheat the slow cooker if necessary. Heat the oil in a large frying pan over a medium heat, add the onion and cook for 4–5 minutes until just beginning to soften. Stir in the ginger, garlic, cumin and coriander seeds.

Place the lentils in a sieve and rinse under cold running water. Drain and transfer to the slow cooker pot. Spoon the onion mixture on top, then add the celery and tomatoes. Pour over the hot stock, season to taste, cover and cook on high for 4–5 hours until the lentils are tender.

Stir in the lemon juice and herbs and spoon into bowls. Top with the yogurt, then scatter with the pomegranate seeds and serve immediately.

For chickpea & lentil tagine, follow the recipe above, adding ½ teaspoon chilli powder with the other spices and using 100 g (3½ oz) Puy lentils and a 400 g (13 oz) can of chickpeas, drained and rinsed, instead of 200 g (7 oz) lentils. Omit the mint and pomegranate, but stir in 25 g (1 oz) parsley and serve topped with the yogurt and a tablespoon of harissa.

Harissa
Red Lentil &
Squash Stew

(VE)

Serves 4
Preparation time 20 minutes
Cooking temperature low
Cooking time 6–8 hours

2 tablespoons extra virgin
  olive oil

1 large onion, finely sliced

4 garlic cloves, finely sliced

1 large butternut squash,
  peeled, deseeded and cut
  into 2 cm (¾ inch) cubes

200 g (7 oz) dried red lentils

1 tablespoon harissa, or more
  to taste

2 teaspoons ground cumin

1 teaspoon ground cinnamon

1 teaspoon ground turmeric

400 g (13 oz) can chopped
  tomatoes

300 ml (½ pint) hot vegan
  bouillon stock

finely grated rind and juice of
  1 unwaxed lemon

salt and pepper

large handful of coriander,
  finely chopped, to serve

This Moroccan stew couldn't be easier to bring together and yet has buckets of flavour. To make it go further, try adding a couple of 400 g (13 oz) cans of chickpeas, drained and rinsed, for the last hour of cooking.

Preheat the slow cooker if necessary. Heat the oil in a large frying pan over a medium heat, add the onion and sauté for about 10 minutes until soft and translucent. Add the garlic and cook for a further minute.

Transfer the onion mixture to the slow cooker and add the butternut squash, lentils, harissa paste, spices, tomatoes and hot stock. Season well with salt and pepper. Cover with the lid and cook on low for 6–8 hours until the squash and lentils are tender and the sauce has thickened.

Season to taste with more harissa and the lemon rind and juice, then serve immediately, sprinkled with the freshly chopped coriander and accompanied by Spicy Tomato & Herb Salad (see below).

For spicy tomato & herb salad, to serve as an accompaniment, thinly slice 4–6 ripe tomatoes and place in a shallow bowl. Add 2 deseeded and finely sliced large green chillies and the finely sliced rind of ½ preserved lemon. Drizzle over a little extra virgin olive or argan oil and season to taste with salt. Gently stir in 1 finely chopped bunch of coriander and serve.

Chillied Beef with Chocolate

Dark chocolate may seem a surprising ingredient in this dish, but it gives depth and richness whilst adding an extra layer of flavour and colour too.

Serves 4
Preparation time 15 minutes
Cooking temperature low
Cooking time 8–10 hours

1 tablespoon sunflower oil

500 g (1 lb) minced beef

1 onion, chopped

3 garlic cloves, finely chopped

1 teaspoon ground cinnamon

1 teaspoon ground cumin

½–1 teaspoon smoked or hot paprika, plus extra to garnish

¼–½ teaspoon crushed dried red chillies

1 bay leaf

400 g (13 oz) can chopped tomatoes

410 g (13½ oz) can red kidney beans, drained and rinsed

2 tablespoons dark muscovado sugar

300 ml (½ pint) beef stock

25 g (1 oz) plain dark chocolate

salt and pepper

soured cream, to serve

Preheat the slow cooker if necessary. Heat the oil in a frying pan, add the beef and onion and fry, stirring, until the mince is evenly browned.

Stir in the garlic, ground spices and bay leaf and cook for 1 minute. Mix in the tomatoes, beans, sugar and stock, then add the chocolate and a little salt and pepper and bring to the boil, stirring.

Pour into the slow cooker pot, cover with the lid and cook on low for 8–10 hours or until cooked through. Stir and spoon on to plates. Top with a little soured cream, Avocado & Red Onion Salsa (see below) and extra paprika. Serve with rice.

For avocado & red onion salsa, to serve as an accompaniment, halve 1 large ripe avocado, remove the stone and peel away the skin. Dice the flesh, then toss in the grated rind and juice of 2 limes. Mix with 1 small finely chopped red onion, 1 chopped tomato and a small bunch of chopped coriander.

Smoky Sweet Potato & Quorn Chilli

Quorn, which is made with mycoprotein, is a versatile low-fat substitute for meat mince in many recipes and works really well in this chipotle-flavoured vegetarian chilli.

Serves 4
Preparation time 20 minutes
Cooking temperature low
Cooking time 7–8 hours

1–2 small dried smoked
　chipotle chillies

4 tablespoons boiling water

low-calorie cooking oil spray

1 onion, chopped

2 garlic cloves, finely chopped

1 teaspoon ground cumin

1 teaspoon paprika

2 x 400 g (13 oz) cans
　chopped tomatoes

400 g (13 oz) can red kidney
　beans, drained and rinsed

1 tablespoon Worcestershire
　sauce (optional)

350 g (11½ oz) Quorn mince

300 g (10 oz) sweet potato, cut
　into 2.5 cm (1 inch) cubes

salt and pepper

For the salsa

½ red onion, finely chopped

3 tablespoons chopped
　coriander

2 tomatoes, halved, deseeded
　and diced

Preheat the slow cooker if necessary. Place the dried chillies in a small bowl, pour over the boiling water and leave to stand for 10 minutes.

Spray a large frying pan with a little low-calorie cooking oil spray and place over a medium heat until hot. Add the onion, fry for 4–5 minutes until softened, then add the garlic, cumin and paprika. Stir in the tomatoes, kidney beans and Worcestershire sauce, if using, then the Quorn and sweet potato. Season to taste.

Finely chop the chillies, then stir into the Quorn mixture with the soaking water. Bring to the boil, stirring, then transfer to the slow cooker pot. Cover and cook on low for 7–8 hours until the sweet potato is tender. Mix the salsa ingredients together, then sprinkle over the chilli to serve.

For sweet potato & soya mince curry, follow the recipe above, omitting the chipotle chillies. Add 1 teaspoon ground turmeric, 1 teaspoon garam masala and ½ teaspoon dried chilli flakes with the cumin and paprika, and a 400 g (13 oz) can lentils, drained and rinsed, when adding the soya mince. Cook as above, then add 100 g (3½ oz) frozen peas and 4 tablespoons chopped coriander, cover again and cook on high for 15 minutes.

Spicy Bean Chilli

This mixed bean chilli is perfect for warming up a long, cold winter's evening. It's very forgiving, so if you forget about it in the slow cooker for a few hours, there is no need to worry.

Serves 8
Preparation time 30 minutes
Cooking temperature low
Cooking time 6 hours

3 tablespoons olive oil

400 g (13 oz) chestnut
    mushrooms, finely chopped

2 onions, finely chopped

1 celery stick, finely chopped

3 garlic cloves, grated

2 teaspoons ground cumin

2 teaspoons ground coriander

1 teaspoon smoked paprika

1 teaspoon dried oregano

1–2 teaspoons hot chilli powder

2 tablespoons plain flour

3 tablespoons tomato purée

2 teaspoons soy sauce

450 ml (¾ pint) hot stock

400 g (13 oz) can chopped
    tomatoes

400 g (13 oz) can red kidney
    beans, drained and rinsed

400 g (13 oz) can mixed
    beans, drained and rinsed

To serve
handful of coriander, chopped
1 lime, cut into wedges

Preheat the slow cooker if necessary. Heat 2 tablespoons of the oil in a large frying pan over a medium heat, add the mushrooms and cook until all the moisture they release has evaporated and they are beginning to turn golden brown. Transfer to the slow cooker.

Add the remaining oil to the frying pan and sauté the onions and celery for about 6 minutes until soft and translucent. Stir in the garlic and cook for a further minute, followed by the spices, cooking for 2 minutes. Add the flour and cook, stirring, for 2 more minutes.

Transfer the onion mixture to the slow cooker and add the tomato purée, soy sauce, hot stock and tomatoes. Cover with the lid and cook on low for 5 hours. Stir in the beans, replace the lid and cook, still on low, for 1 hour.

Season to taste and serve immediately, sprinkled with finely chopped coriander and with lime wedges for squeezing over, along with some Tomato & Chilli Salsa (see below) and rice or bread.

For tomato & chilli salsa, to serve as an accompaniment, place 500 g (1 lb) chopped tomatoes, 1 finely chopped red chilli (deseeded, if liked), 1 finely chopped garlic clove, 1 finely chopped small onion, 2 tablespoons tomato purée, 2 tablespoons red wine vinegar and 1 tablespoon sugar in a bowl and mix well.

Gourmet Bolognese

Everyday spag bol goes posh with this gourmet version which adds pancetta, chicken livers and red wine for a meal that's hard to beat.

Serves 4
Preparation time 20 minutes
Cooking temperature low
Cooking time 8–10 hours

1 tablespoon olive oil

500 g (1 lb) lean minced beef

1 onion, chopped

225 g (7½ oz) chicken livers, thawed if frozen

2 garlic cloves, finely chopped

50 g (2 oz) pancetta or smoked back bacon rashers, diced

150 g (5 oz) cup mushrooms, sliced

1 tablespoon plain flour

150 ml (¼ pint) red wine

150 ml (¼ pint) beef stock

400 g (13 oz) can chopped tomatoes

2 tablespoons tomato purée

1 bouquet garni

salt and pepper

300 g (10 oz) dried tagliatelle

To serve
Parmesan cheese shavings
basil leaves

Preheat the slow cooker if necessary. Heat the oil in a frying pan, add the mince and onion and fry, stirring and breaking up the mince with a wooden spoon, until it is evenly browned.

Meanwhile, rinse the chicken livers in a sieve, drain and then chop roughly, discarding any white cores. Add to the frying pan with the garlic, pancetta or bacon and mushrooms and cook for 2–3 minutes or until the chicken livers are browned.

Stir in the flour, then mix in the wine, stock, tomatoes, tomato purée, bouquet garni and seasoning. Bring to the boil, stirring. Spoon into the slow cooker pot, cover with the lid and cook on low for 8–10 hours.

When almost ready to serve, cook the tagliatelle in a large saucepan of lightly salted boiling water according to the packet instructions until just tender. Drain and stir into the Bolognese sauce. Spoon into shallow bowls and sprinkle with Parmesan shavings and some basil leaves.

For budget Bolognese, omit the chicken livers and pancetta or bacon and add 1 diced carrot and 1 diced courgette along with the garlic and mushrooms. Replace the wine with extra stock and continue as above.

Meat-free Mushroom Bolognese

This meat-free Bolognese recipe is slow cooked and packed full of flavour. The use of mushrooms and walnuts adds a 'meaty' flavour to the dish, making it similar to the original.

Serves 6
Preparation time 25 minutes
Cooking temperature high
Cooking time 4 hours

2 tablespoons olive oil
1 onion, finely chopped
2 carrots, finely chopped
1 celery stick, finely chopped
3 garlic cloves, crushed
1 teaspoon fennel seeds
450 g (14½ oz) chestnut
    mushrooms, finely chopped
125 g (4 oz) walnuts
2 tablespoons tomato purée
1 teaspoon dried oregano
200 ml (7 fl oz) red wine
2 x 400 g (13 oz) cans
    chopped tomatoes
500 ml (17 fl oz) vegetable or
    mushroom stock
1 teaspoon soy sauce
1 bay leaf
salt and pepper

To serve
basil leaves
grated vegetarian Italian hard
    cheese

Preheat the slow cooker if necessary. Heat the oil in a large frying pan, add the onion, carrots and celery and cook over a medium heat for about 8 minutes until softened. Stir in the garlic, fennel seeds and mushrooms and cook for about 5 minutes until the mushrooms are golden brown and the liquid released from the mushrooms has evaporated.

Meanwhile, place the walnuts in a food processor and process until finely chopped. Alternatively, finely chop with a sharp knife.

Transfer the mushroom mixture to the slow cooker, add the chopped walnuts and all the remaining ingredients and mix together. Cover with the lid and cook on high for 4 hours until the sauce has reduced and thickened. Season well with salt and pepper and remove the bay leaf.

Serve hot with cooked tagliatelle or spaghetti, sprinkled with a few basil leaves and a grating of cheese.

Vegan Bolognese

VE

This meat-free version of the famous Italian sauce is not only perfect for enjoying with pasta, but makes a great alternative base for a vegan shepherd's pie. The food processor can be your helpful assistant in this recipe, blitzing any vegetable that calls for being 'finely chopped' to save on prep time.

Serves 4–6
Preparation time 25 minutes
Cooking temperature low
Cooking time 7–8 hours

3 tablespoons olive oil

1 onion, finely chopped

1 celery stick, finely chopped

1 large carrot, finely chopped

1 garlic clove, finely chopped

25 g (1 oz) dried porcini mushrooms, crumbled or roughly chopped

150 ml (¼ pint) boiling water

300 g (10 oz) chestnut mushrooms, finely chopped

50 g (2 oz) dried red lentils

50 g (2 oz) dried green lentils

400 g (13 oz) can chopped tomatoes

1 tablespoon tomato purée

3 thyme sprigs, leaves picked

2 teaspoons Marmite

1 tablespoon balsamic vinegar,

300 ml (½ pint) hot stock

To serve
450 g (14½ oz) dried spaghetti

Grated hard vegan cheese

fresh basil leaves

Preheat the slow cooker if necessary. Heat the oil in a large frying pan over a medium-low heat, add the onion, celery and carrot with a pinch of salt and sauté for 5–10 minutes until beginning to soften and colour. Add the garlic and sauté for a further minute.

Meanwhile, put the porcini mushrooms into the slow cooker, pour over the measured boiling water and leave to soak.

Transfer the onion mixture to the slow cooker and add all the remaining ingredients. Cover with the lid and cook on low for 7–8 hours. Check and season to taste, perhaps adding a dash more vinegar if needed.

When ready to serve, cook the spaghetti in a large saucepan of salted boiling water according to the packet instructions. Drain and toss with the sauce. Serve immediately, with some hard vegan cheese grated over, garnished with a few basil leaves.

Olive & Lemon Meatballs

Serves 4
Preparation time 30 minutes
Cooking temperature low
Cooking time 6–8 hours

For the meatballs
50 g (2 oz) pitted black olives,
    chopped
grated rind of ½ lemon
500 g (1 lb) extra-lean minced
    beef
1 egg yolk
1 tablespoon olive oil

For the sauce
1 onion, chopped
2 garlic cloves, finely chopped
400 g (13 oz) can chopped
    tomatoes
1 teaspoon caster sugar
150 ml (¼ pint) chicken stock
salt and pepper
small basil leaves, to garnish

You can't beat a comforting bowl of pasta with meatballs, and these ones have lovely Mediterranean flavours of lemon and olive. They freeze well uncooked so you can make a double batch for one supper now and another later.

Preheat the slow cooker if necessary. Put all the ingredients for the meatballs except for the oil in a bowl and mix with a wooden spoon. Wet your hands and shape the mixture into 20 balls.

Heat the oil in a large frying pan, add the meatballs and cook over a high heat, turning, until browned on all sides. Lift them out of pan with a slotted spoon and transfer to a plate.

Make the sauce. Add the onion to the pan and fry, stirring, for 5 minutes or until lightly browned. Add the garlic, tomatoes, sugar, stock and salt and pepper and bring to the boil, stirring.

Transfer the meatballs to the slow cooker pot, pour over the hot sauce, cover and cook on low for 6–8 hours. Garnish with basil leaves and serve with tagliatelle tossed with chopped basil and melted butter.

For herb & garlic meatballs, replace the olives and lemon rind with 2 finely chopped garlic cloves and 3 tablespoons chopped basil leaves. Mix, shape and cook the meatballs with the sauce as above, adding a small handful of basil leaves to the sauce just before serving.

Tandoori Chicken

Watching your weight needn't mean missing out on your favourite dishes as this delicious but light take on the classic Indian dish proves.

Serves 4
Preparation time 20 minutes, plus marinating
Cooking temperature high
Cooking time 3–4 hours

150 ml (¼ pint) fat-free Greek yogurt
4 cm (1½ inch) piece of fresh root ginger, peeled and grated
3 tablespoons chopped coriander leaves
3 teaspoons medium-hot curry powder
½ teaspoon ground turmeric
1 teaspoon paprika
625 g (1¼ lb) boneless, skinless chicken thighs, cut into chunks
juice of ½ lemon
low-calorie cooking oil spray
salt and pepper

To serve
50 g (2 oz) mixed green salad leaves
¼ cucumber, diced
small handful of coriander leaves
juice of ½ lemon

Place the yogurt in a mixing bowl and stir in the ginger, coriander, curry powder, turmeric and paprika. Toss the chicken with the lemon juice, season lightly and stir into the yogurt mixture until evenly coated. Cover the bowl and chill overnight.

Preheat the slow cooker if necessary. Stir the chicken mixture, then transfer to the slow cooker pot in an even layer. Cover and cook on high for 3–4 hours or until the chicken is tender and cooked through. (The yogurt will separate during cooking but this will not affect the taste.)

Spray a large frying pan with a little low-calorie cooking oil spray and place over a high heat until hot. Transfer the chicken to the frying pan, a few pieces at a time until all the chicken is in the pan, and cook for 2–3 minutes, turning once, until golden on both sides. This step can be omitted if you are short of time.

Toss the salad leaves, cucumber and coriander leaves with the lemon juice, arrange on serving plates and top with the chicken.

For garlicky tandoori chicken, add 3 finely chopped garlic cloves to the yogurt and spice mixture and continue as above.

Chicken & Sweet Potato Balti

Just six ingredients and a few minutes prep are all it takes to make a fantastic curry – you'll be coming back to this recipe time and time again.

Serves 4
Preparation time 15 minutes
Cooking temperature high and low
Cooking time 5½–6½ hours

6 boneless, skinless chicken thighs, about 500 g (1 lb) in total, cubed
1 onion, sliced
375 g (12 oz) sweet potatoes, cut into 2 cm (¾ inch) cubes
2 garlic cloves, finely chopped
425 g (14 oz) jar balti curry sauce
roughly chopped coriander, to garnish (optional)

Preheat the slow cooker if necessary. Arrange the chicken, onion and sweet potatoes in the base of the slow cooker pot in an even layer. Sprinkle with the chopped garlic.

Bring the curry sauce just to the boil in a small saucepan or the microwave. Pour into the slow cooker pot in an even layer. Cover with the lid and cook on high for 30 minutes. Reduce the heat and cook on low for 5½–6½ hours, until the chicken is cooked through and the sauce piping hot.

Stir well, then sprinkle with roughly chopped coriander, if liked. Spoon into bowls and serve with warmed naan bread.

For harissa baked chicken with sweet potato, prepare the chicken and vegetables as above. Replace the balti curry sauce with a 400 g (13 oz) can chopped tomatoes and 2 teaspoons harissa. Continue as above.

Kashmiri Butter Chicken

Serves 4
Preparation time 30 minutes
Cooking temperature low
Cooking time 5–7 hours

2 onions, quartered

3 garlic cloves

3.5 cm (1½ inch) piece of fresh
   root ginger, peeled

1 large red chilli, deseeded

8 boneless, skinless chicken
   thighs

1 tablespoon sunflower oil

25 g (1 oz) butter

1 teaspoon cumin seeds,
   crushed

1 teaspoon fennel seeds,
   crushed

4 cardamom pods, crushed

1 teaspoon paprika

1 teaspoon ground turmeric

¼ teaspoon ground cinnamon

300 ml (½ pint) chicken stock

1 tablespoon brown sugar

2 tablespoons tomato purée

5 tablespoons double cream

salt

To garnish
toasted flaked almonds
coriander sprigs

Skip the takeaway this weekend and make your own version of an Indian favourite with this simple but flavour-packed butter chicken recipe.

Preheat the slow cooker if necessary. Blend the onions, garlic, ginger and chilli in a food processor or blender, or chop finely.

Cut each chicken thigh into 4 pieces. Heat the oil in a large frying pan and add the chicken a few pieces at a time until all the meat has been added. Cook over a high heat until browned. Drain and transfer to a plate.

Add the butter to the frying pan. When it has melted, add the onion paste and cook over a more moderate heat until it is just beginning to colour. Stir in the crushed cumin and fennel seeds, the cardamom pods and their black seeds and ground spices. Cook for 1 minute, then mix in the stock, sugar, tomato purée and salt. Bring to the boil, stirring.

Transfer the chicken to the slow cooker pot, pour the onion mixture and sauce over the top and press the pieces of chicken below the surface of the liquid. Cover with the lid and cook on low for 5–7 hours.

Stir in the cream. Garnish with toasted flaked almonds and coriander sprigs and serve with boiled rice and Coriander Flat Breads (see below).

For coriander flat breads, to serve as an accompaniment, mix together 200 g (7 oz) self-raising flour, ½ teaspoon baking powder, 3 tablespoons roughly chopped coriander leaves and a little salt in a bowl. Add 2 tablespoons sunflower oil, then gradually mix in 6–7 tablespoons water to make a soft dough. Cut the dough into 4 pieces and roll out each piece thinly on a lightly floured surface to form a rough oval. Cook on a preheated ridged griddle pan for 3–4 minutes on each side until singed and puffy.

Tofu Tikka Masala

This curry packs a powerful punch of flavour. Swap the tofu for cauliflower or any other vegetable if you're not a tofu fan, but you're guaranteed to be mopping up every last bit of this rich sauce.

Serves 6–8
Preparation time 20 minutes
Cooking temperature low
Cooking time 7–9 hours

2 x 400 g (13 oz) cans
 chopped tomatoes
2 tablespoons coconut oil
4 garlic cloves, finely chopped
20 g (¾ oz) fresh root ginger,
 peeled and finely grated
6–8 cardamom pods (use
 black cardamom if available)
2 cinnamon sticks
1 tablespoon garam masala
1 teaspoon ground cumin
½ teaspoon chilli powder
½ teaspoon ground turmeric
500 g (1 lb) silken tofu, drained
 and cut into 2.5 cm (1 inch)
 cubes
1 teaspoon dried fenugreek
 leaves (methi), crumbled
2 tablespoons sugar
200 ml (7 fl oz) coconut cream
salt and pepper

To serve
small handful of coriander
1 lemon, cut into wedges

Preheat the slow cooker if necessary. Blitz the tomatoes in a food processor until smooth. Transfer to the slow cooker.

Heat the coconut oil in a frying pan over a medium heat, and the garlic and ginger and sauté for about 3 minutes until fragrant and golden. Stir in the cardamom pods, cinnamon sticks and ground spices and cook for a further minute.

Transfer the spice mixture to the slow cooker, cover with the lid and cook on low for 6–8 hours. Stir in the tofu cubes, fenugreek leaves, sugar and coconut cream, replace the lid and cook on high for 1 hour.

Season to taste with salt and pepper and serve immediately, sprinkled with the coriander leaves and with lemon wedges for squeezing over, along with Simple Pilau Rice (see below) on the side.

For simple pilau rice, to serve as an accompaniment, place 1 tablespoon mild curry powder in a medium saucepan with 4 crushed green cardamom pods, 1 cinnamon stick, 2 cloves and 300 g (10 oz) basmati rice. Add 650 ml (1 pint 2 fl oz) boiling water, season with salt and pepper and bring to the boil. Reduce the heat to low, cover the pan and cook gently for 10–12 minutes or until all the water has been absorbed. Remove from the heat and allow to stand, covered and undisturbed, for 10–15 minutes. Fluff up the grains with a fork and serve.

Oriental Pork with Pak Choi

(DF)

This low-fat dish has a glorious, beautifully balanced broth redolent with big-hitter flavours including star anise, fish sauce and chilli and ginger.

Serves 4
Preparation time 20 minutes
Cooking temperature low and high
Cooking time 6¼–7¼ hours

4 pork medallions, 350 g (11½ oz) in total
1 red onion, thinly sliced
2.5 cm (1 inch) piece of fresh root ginger, peeled and thinly sliced
1 garlic clove, thinly sliced
small handful of coriander leaves
¼ teaspoon dried chilli flakes
2 small star anise
1 teaspoon Thai fish sauce (nam pla)
2 teaspoons tomato purée
4 teaspoons dark soy sauce
350 ml (12 fl oz) hot chicken stock
200 g (7 oz) pak choi, thickly sliced
100 g (3½ oz) asparagus tips
250 g (8 oz) dried egg noodles, to serve

Preheat the slow cooker if necessary. Place the pork medallions in the slow cooker pot in a single layer and scatter with the onion, ginger and garlic. Sprinkle half the coriander leaves on top.

Stir the chilli flakes, star anise, fish sauce, tomato purée and soy sauce into the hot chicken stock, then pour over the pork. Cover and cook on low for 6–7 hours until the pork is tender.

Add the pak choi and asparagus to the slow cooker pot, cover and cook on high for 15 minutes until the vegetables are just tender and still bright green.

Meanwhile, cook the egg noodles in a saucepan of lightly salted boiling water according to packet instructions until tender. Drain and divide between 4 bowls, top with the pork and vegetables, then spoon over the broth and serve garnished with the remaining coriander.

For Oriental pork with mixed vegetables, follow the recipe above, adding 300 g (10 oz) ready-prepared mixed stir-fry vegetables instead of the pak choi and asparagus.

Pork with Black Bean Sauce

(DF)

This slow-cooker version of a Sichuan favourite couldn't be easier. Just remember to marinate the pork steaks overnight for maximum flavour and succulence.

Serves 4
Preparation time 20 minutes, plus overnight marinating
Cooking temperature high and low
Cooking time 7½–9½ hours

4 spare rib pork steaks, about 175 g (6 oz) each
2 tablespoons cornflour
4 tablespoons soy sauce
3.5 cm (1½ inch) piece of fresh root ginger, peeled and finely chopped
2 garlic cloves, finely chopped
100 g (3½ oz) black bean sauce
300 ml (½ pint) boiling chicken stock
pepper

To serve
1 tablespoon sunflower oil
300 g (10 oz) ready-prepared mixed stir-fry vegetables
cooked rice

Put the pork steaks into a shallow non-metallic dish. Put the cornflour and soy sauce in a small bowl and mix to a smooth paste, then add the ginger, garlic, black bean sauce and a little pepper. Pour over the pork, cover with clingfilm and marinate in the refrigerator overnight.

Preheat the slow cooker if necessary. Put the pork and marinade into the slow cooker pot. Pour over the boiling stock, cover with the lid and cook on high for 30 minutes. Reduce the heat and cook on low for 7½–9½ hours, until the pork is cooked through and tender.

When almost ready to serve, heat the oil in a large frying pan, add the mixed vegetables and stir-fry for 2–3 minutes or until just tender. Spoon the pork on to plates lined with rice and top with the vegetables.

For sweet & sour pork, omit the black bean sauce from the marinade and add the marinated pork to the slow cooker pot with a bunch of sliced spring onions, 1 cored, deseeded and sliced red pepper and 100 g (3½ oz) sliced mushrooms. Replace the chicken stock with a 425 g (14 oz) jar sweet and sour sauce. Bring the sauce to the boil in a saucepan or the microwave, then pour into the slow cooker pot. Continue as above.

Tamarind Beef with Ginger Beer

Ginger beer is the surprising special ingredient in this dish with its delectable sweet-sour note of tamarind and hint of chilli heat.

Serves 4
Preparation time 20 minutes
Cooking temperature low
Cooking time 8–10 hours

2 tablespoons sunflower oil

750 g (1½ lb) lean stewing beef, cubed

1 onion, chopped

2 garlic cloves, finely chopped

2 tablespoons plain flour

330 ml (11½ fl oz) can ginger beer

6 teaspoons tamarind paste

½ teaspoon crushed dried red chillies

1 teaspoon ground mixed spice

1 tablespoon dark muscovado sugar

salt and pepper

Preheat the slow cooker if necessary. Heat the oil in a large frying pan, add the beef a few pieces at a time until all the pieces are in the pan, then add the onion and fry over a medium heat, stirring, until the meat is evenly browned.

Stir in the garlic and flour. Gradually mix in the ginger beer, then stir in the tamarind paste, dried chillies and spice, sugar and a little salt and pepper and bring to the boil, stirring.

Transfer to the slow cooker pot and press the beef below the surface of the liquid. Cover with the lid and cook on low for 8–10 hours or until the meat is cooked through and tender.

Stir the beef, then ladle into bowls and top with Garlic & Coriander Croutes (see below) and serve with steamed broccoli.

For ginger & coriander croutes, to serve as an accompaniment, heat 2 cm (¾ inch) piece peeled and grated root ginger with 2 finely chopped garlic cloves and 50 g (2 oz) butter, stir in ½ mild, deseeded, finely chopped red chilli or a large pinch of dried crushed chillies, 3 tablespoons chopped coriander leaves and a little salt and pepper. Toast 8 slices of French stick on both sides and spread with the butter while hot. Arrange the croutes on top of the casserole and serve immediately.

Asian Glazed Ribs

(DF)

Slathered in a finger-licking sticky glaze, slow cooking produces the best, fall-off-the-bone ribs you'll ever eat!

Serves 4
Preparation time 25 minutes, plus overnight marinating
Cooking temperature high and low
Cooking time 7½–9½ hours

1 onion, quartered

5 cm (2 inches) fresh root ginger, peeled and sliced

2 tablespoons rice or white wine vinegar

4 star anise

1 cinnamon stick, halved

1.25 kg (2½ lb) pork ribs

1 litre (1¾ pints) boiling water

2 breakfast tea bags

For the glaze

4 tablespoons runny honey

4 tablespoons soy sauce

Put the onion, ginger, vinegar, star anise and cinnamon into a bowl and cover with clingfilm. Chill in the refrigerator overnight.

Preheat the slow cooker if necessary. Pour the boiling water over the teabags and leave to brew for 2–3 minutes, then squeeze out the bags and discard. Rinse the ribs with cold water, drain and put into the slow cooker pot with the spiced onion mix and the hot tea.

Cover with the lid and cook on high for 30 minutes. Reduce the heat and cook on low for 7½–9½ hours, until the meat is almost falling off the bones.

Lift the ribs out of the slow cooker pot and transfer to a foil-lined grill pan. Put 6 tablespoons of stock from the pot into a bowl and mix in the honey and soy sauce. Spoon over the ribs, then grill for 10–15 minutes, turning several times and spooning soy mixture over until browned and glazed. Serve with Pickled Cucumber (see below) and rice.

For pickled cucumber, to serve as an accompaniment, mix ¼–½ mild red chilli, deseeded and finely chopped, 3 tablespoons chopped coriander, 1 tablespoon rice or white wine vinegar, 1 teaspoon fish sauce (nam pla) and ½ teaspoon caster sugar in a salad bowl. Very thinly slice ½ cucumber, add to the dressing and toss together gently. This dish can be made ahead of time, covered with clingfilm and kept in the refrigerator overnight.

Baked Seafood with Saffron

Golden saffron imparts a lovely colour and flavour to this pasta dish which is a great recipe to have in your arsenal for informal entertaining. You can use spaghetti or linguine in place of the tagliatelle.

Serves 4
Preparation time 15 minutes
Cooking temperature low and high
Cooking time 5½–7½ hours

1 onion, finely chopped

1 red pepper, cored, deseeded and diced

2 garlic cloves, finely chopped

400 g (13 oz) can chopped tomatoes

150 ml (¼ pint) dry white wine or fish stock

large pinch of saffron threads

2 thyme sprigs

1 tablespoon olive oil

400 g (13 oz) pack frozen seafood (prawns, mussels, squid), thawed

300 g (10 oz) dried tagliatelle

salt and pepper

chopped parsley, to serve

Preheat the slow cooker if necessary. Put the onion, red pepper, garlic and tomatoes into the slow cooker pot, then add the wine or stock, saffron, thyme, oil and a little salt and pepper.

Cover with the lid and cook on low for 5–7 hours. Rinse the seafood with cold water, drain and then stir into the slow cooker pot. Replace the lid and cook on high for 30 minutes or until piping hot.

When almost ready to serve, cook the tagliatelle in a large saucepan of lightly salted boiling water according to the packet instructions until just tender. Drain and toss with chopped parsley. Spoon into shallow bowls and top with the seafood sauce.

For baked salmon with pesto, omit the seafood and drain a 400 g (13 oz) can red salmon, remove the skin and bones and break the fish into large flakes. Put the onion, red pepper and garlic into the slow cooker pot. Heat the tomatoes and wine or stock in a small saucepan or the microwave, then add to the pot with 2 teaspoons pesto and the oil, omitting the saffron and thyme. Mix in the salmon and continue as above.

Moroccan Meatballs

Leaner than beef or lamb, these healthy meatballs are made with turkey and lentils and are full of juicy flavour and spices.

Serves 4
Preparation time 30 minutes
Cooking temperature low
Cooking time 6–8 hours

500 g (1 lb) minced turkey

100 g (3½ oz) drained and rinsed canned green lentils

1 egg yolk

1 tablespoon olive oil

1 onion, sliced

2 garlic cloves, finely chopped

1 teaspoon turmeric

1 teaspoon ground coriander

½ teaspoon ground cumin

½ teaspoon ground cinnamon

2.5 cm (1 inch) fresh root ginger, peeled and finely chopped

400 g (13 oz) can chopped tomatoes

150 ml (¼ pint) chicken stock

salt and pepper

Preheat the slow cooker if necessary. Mix together the minced turkey, green lentils, a little salt and pepper and the egg yolk in a bowl or food processor. Divide into 20 pieces, then shape into small balls with wetted hands.

Heat the oil in a large frying pan, add the meatballs and fry, stirring, until browned but not cooked through. Lift out of the pan with a slotted spoon and put into the slow cooker pot. Add the onion and fry until softened, then stir in the garlic, spices and ginger and cook for 1 minute.

Stir in the tomatoes, stock and a little salt and pepper and bring to the boil, stirring. Pour over the meatballs, cover with the lid and cook on low for 6–8 hours or until cooked through. Stir, then spoon on to couscous-lined plates (see below).

For lemon couscous, to accompany the meatballs, put 200 g (7 oz) couscous into a bowl, pour over 450 ml (¾ pint) boiling water, the grated rind and juice of 1 lemon, 2 tablespoons olive oil and some salt and pepper. Cover and leave to stand for 5 minutes. Fluff up with a fork and stir in a small bunch of chopped coriander.

Tapenade-topped Cod

DF

Easy to make, low in calories and packed with Mediterranean flavours, this is a great healthy choice. The tapenade topping works brilliantly with all white fish and with chicken too.

Serves 4
Preparation time 15 minutes
Cooking temperature low
Cooking time 3½–4 hours

200 g (7 oz) passata
200 g (7 oz) spinach, rinsed
    and drained
175 g (6 oz) tomatoes, roughly
    chopped
50 g (2 oz) chorizo, diced
4 skinless cod steaks, 150 g
    (5 oz) each
85 g (3¼ oz) green olives
    stuffed with hot pimento
small handful of basil leaves,
    plus extra to garnish
salt and pepper

Preheat the slow cooker if necessary. Spoon the passata over the base of the slow cooker pot, then arrange the spinach, tomatoes and chorizo in an even layer on top. Season to taste and place the fish steaks on top in a single layer, then season again.

Place the olives and basil in a food processor and blitz until finely chopped, or chop with a knife. Spread the mixture over the cod steaks, then cover and cook on low for 3½ –4 hours until the fish is bright white and flakes easily when pressed with a small knife. Serve garnished with extra basil.

For herb-topped cod, mix 15 g (½ oz) finely chopped parsley and 15 g (½ oz) finely chopped basil with ½ teaspoon crushed cumin seeds and the grated rind of 1 lemon. Follow the recipe above, using this herb mixture to spread over the cod steaks before cooking instead of the olives and basil.

Indian Spiced Cottage Pie

(DF)

A wonderful alternative to traditional cottage pie, this version adds warming spices and sweet sultanas to create a dish that all the family will love.

Serves 4
Preparation time 30 minutes
Cooking temperature low
Cooking time 8–10 hours

1 tablespoon sunflower oil

500 g (1 lb) lean minced beef

1 onion, chopped

4 tablespoons korma curry
   paste

1 teaspoon ground turmeric

2 carrots, diced

2 tablespoons plain flour

100 g (3½ oz) dried red lentils,
   rinsed and drained

50 g (2 oz) sultanas

1 tablespoon tomato purée

900 ml (1½ pints) beef stock

salt and pepper

For the topping

875 g (1¾ lb) potatoes, cut into
   chunks

50 g (2 oz) butter

3 tablespoons milk

1 tablespoon sunflower oil

bunch of spring onions,
   chopped

½ teaspoon ground turmeric

Preheat the slow cooker if necessary. Heat the oil in a large frying pan, add the mince and onion and cook, stirring and breaking up the meat, until it is evenly browned. Stir in the curry paste and turmeric and cook for 1 minute. Stir in the carrots and flour, then add the lentils, sultanas, tomato purée, stock and salt and pepper. Bring to the boil, stirring, then pour into the slow cooker pot. Cover with the lid and cook on low for 8–10 hours or until the lentils are soft and the beef is tender.

When almost ready to serve, put the potatoes in a saucepan of boiling water and simmer for 15 minutes or until tender. Drain and mash with half the butter, the milk and salt and pepper. Heat the oil in a frying pan, add the spring onions and fry for 2–3 minutes or until softened. Add the turmeric and cook for 1 minute, then mix into the mash.

Stir the beef mixture and lift the pot out of the slow cooker using oven gloves. Transfer to a serving dish, if liked. Spoon the mash on top, dot with remaining butter, then place under a preheated medium grill until golden. Serve with cooked peas.

For traditional cottage pie, fry the beef and onion as above. Omit the curry paste and turmeric. Add the carrots and flour, then replace the lentils and sultanas with a 410 g (13½ oz) can baked beans, 1 tablespoon each tomato purée and Worcestershire sauce, 300 ml (½ pint) beef stock and 1 teaspoon dried mixed herbs. Transfer to the slow cooker pot and continue as above. Top with the mash, omitting the spring onions and turmeric. Sprinkle with 50 g (2 oz) grated Cheddar cheese and place under a preheated hot grill until browned.

Chicken Cacciatore

 DF L

The classic 'hunter's stew' – 'cacciatore' means 'hunter' in Italian – gets a health makeover in this tasty but low-calorie dish.

Serves 4
Preparation time 20 minutes
Cooking temperature low
Cooking time 8–9 hours

low-calorie cooking oil spray

500 g (1 lb) boneless, skinless chicken thighs, cubed

1 onion, chopped

2 garlic cloves, finely chopped

1 red pepper, cored, deseeded and diced

1 orange pepper, cored, deseeded and diced

2 celery sticks, diced

150 ml (¼ pint) chicken stock

400 g (13 oz) can chopped tomatoes

1 tablespoon tomato purée

1 tablespoon balsamic vinegar

leaves from 2 rosemary sprigs, chopped

200 g (7 oz) dried tagliatelle

salt and pepper

2 tablespoons chopped parsley, to garnish

Preheat the slow cooker if necessary. Spray a large frying pan with a little low-calorie cooking oil spray and place over a high heat until hot. Add the chicken a few pieces at a time until all the chicken is in the pan and cook for 3–4 minutes, stirring, until just beginning to brown. Add the onion and continue to cook until the chicken is golden and the onion has softened.

Stir in the garlic, peppers and celery, then add the stock, tomatoes, tomato purée, balsamic vinegar and rosemary. Season generously and bring to the boil, stirring. Transfer to the slow cooker pot, cover and cook on low for 8–9 hours until the chicken is tender and cooked through.

When almost ready to serve, cook the tagliatelle in a large saucepan of lightly salted boiling water according to the packet instructions until just tender. Drain, then toss with the chicken mixture and serve garnished with the parsley.

For potato-topped cacciatore, follow the recipe above and place all the ingredients in the slow cooker pot. Thinly slice 625 g (1¼ lb) potatoes and arrange them on top of the chicken mixture, overlapping. Press the potatoes down into the liquid, then cover and cook on high for 5–6 hours until the potatoes and chicken are cooked through. If liked, lift the pot out of the slow cooker using oven gloves, spray the potatoes with a little extra low-calorie cooking oil spray and place under a preheated hot grill until the potatoes are golden.

Creamy Wild Mushroom Stroganoff

This vegetarian stroganoff is full of beautiful wild mushrooms, which give the dish depth and a real 'meaty' and earthy flavour.

Serves 4
Preparation time 35 minutes, plus soaking
Cooking temperature low
Cooking time 4 hours

15 g (½ oz) dried porcini mushrooms
400 ml (14 fl oz) boiling water
50 g (2 oz) unsalted butter
400 g (13 oz) shallots, sliced
3 garlic cloves, sliced
2 tablespoons thyme leaves
400 g (13 oz) portobello mushrooms, sliced
300 g (10 oz) shiitake mushrooms, halved
200 g (7 oz) oyster mushrooms, sliced lengthways
100 ml (3½ fl oz) white wine
1 tablespoon wholegrain mustard
1 teaspoon vegetarian Worcestershire sauce
150 ml (¼ pint) soured cream
small handful of parsley, chopped, plus extra to garnish
salt and pepper

Preheat the slow cooker if necessary. Put the porcini mushrooms into a small heatproof bowl and pour over the measured water. Leave to soak until rehydrated.

Meanwhile, heat the butter in a large frying pan, add the shallots and cook over a low heat for about 8 minutes until very soft and translucent. Stir in the garlic and thyme and fry for a few minutes until softened. Add the portobello, shiitake and oyster mushrooms and cook over a medium heat for a further 5 minutes until beginning to soften and caramelize. Pour in the wine and bring to the boil, then reduce the heat and simmer for 1 minute.

Transfer the mushroom mixture to the slow cooker, add the porcini mushrooms and their soaking water, the mustard and Worcestershire sauce and mix together. Season well with salt and pepper.

Cover with the lid and cook on low for 4 hours until the sauce has thickened. Stir in the soured cream and parsley and adjust the seasoning to taste. Garnish with a little more chopped parsley and serve with cooked rice or pasta.

Tarragon Chicken with Mushrooms

Tarragon has a sweet and subtle aniseed flavour and pairs beautifully with the chicken in this light dish, ideal for a midweek supper.

Serves 4
Preparation time 20 minutes
Cooking temperature high
Cooking time 8¼–9½ hours

low-calorie cooking oil spray

4 skinless chicken legs, 1.2 kg (2 lb 6 oz) in total

2 leeks, trimmed and sliced

175 g (6 oz) closed-cap mushrooms, sliced

1 tablespoon plain flour

1 teaspoon mustard powder

450 ml (¾ pint) chicken stock

2 tablespoons chopped tarragon, plus extra to garnish

3 tablespoons sherry (optional)

125 g (4 oz) fine green beans

salt and pepper

Preheat the slow cooker if necessary. Spray a large frying pan with a little low-calorie cooking oil spray and place over a high heat until hot. Add the chicken legs and cook for 4–5 minutes, turning once, until golden. Transfer to the slow cooker pot.

Add a little extra low-calorie cooking oil spray to the pan if necessary, then add the white leek slices (reserving the green slices) and the mushrooms and cook for 2–3 minutes. Stir in the flour, then add the mustard powder, stock, tarragon and sherry, if using. Season to taste and bring to the boil, stirring.

Pour the liquid and vegetables over the chicken, cover and cook on low for 8–9 hours until the chicken is tender and cooked through.

Stir the casserole, then add the remaining green leek slices and the green beans. Cover again and cook on high for 15–30 minutes until the vegetables are tender. Spoon into shallow bowls and serve garnished with a little extra tarragon.

For low-cal garlicky mash, to serve as an accompaniment, peel and cut 625 g (1¼ lb) potatoes into chunks and cook in a saucepan of lightly salted boiling water for about 15 minutes until tender. Drain and mash with 3 tablespoons chicken stock, 2 crushed garlic cloves and a little salt and pepper.

Braised Duck with Orange Sauce

(DF)

There's a reason this retro dish is a classic – it's delicious. For a more intense orange flavour, try adding a dollop of Seville orange marmalade to the sauce before pouring it over the duck.

Serves 4
Preparation time 15 minutes
Cooking temperature high
Cooking time 4–5 hours

4 duck legs, about 175 g (6 oz) each

1 onion, sliced

2 tablespoons plain flour

150 ml (¼ pint) chicken stock

150 ml (¼ pint) dry white wine

1 large orange, half sliced, half squeezed juice

1 bay leaf

1 teaspoon Dijon mustard

salt

½ teaspoon black peppercorns, roughly crushed

Preheat the slow cooker if necessary. Dry-fry the duck in a large frying pan over a low heat until the fat begins to run, then increase the heat until the duck is browned on both sides. Lift out of the pan with a slotted spoon and transfer to the slow cooker pot.

Pour off any excess fat to leave about 1 tablespoon. Fry the onions until softened. Stir in the flour, then mix in the stock, wine, orange juice, bay leaf, a little salt and the crushed peppercorns and bring to the boil, stirring. Add the sliced orange.

Pour the sauce over the duck, cover with the lid and cook on high for 4–5 hours or until the duck is tender and almost falling off the bones. Serve with rice and steamed green beans.

For braised duck with cranberries & port, fry the duck and onions as above. Mix in the flour and stock, then replace the wine with 150 ml (¼ pint) ruby port and 100 g (3½ oz) fresh cranberries. Add orange slices and juice and continue as above.

Tomato Braised Squid with Chorizo

(DF)

The secret of succulent squid is to cook it either very fast in a frying pan or very slowly, as here, with wine and tomatoes. The chorizo adds a depth and spiciness to the sauce.

Serves 4
Preparation time 20 minutes
Cooking temperature low
Cooking time 3½ –5½ hours

625 g (1¼ lb) chilled squid

1 onion, thinly sliced

125 g (4 oz) ready-diced chorizo

125 g (4 oz) closed-cup mushrooms, sliced

1 red pepper, cored, deseeded and sliced

2 garlic cloves, finely chopped

2–3 sprigs of rosemary, leaves stripped from the stems

1 tablespoon tomato purée

1 teaspoon caster sugar

400 g (13 oz) can chopped tomatoes

100 ml (3½ fl oz) red wine

1 tablespoon cornflour

salt and pepper

chopped parsley, to garnish

Preheat the slow cooker if necessary. Rinse the squid inside and out, pulling out the tentacles and reserving. Drain and slice the bodies. Put the tentacles in a bowl, cover with clingfilm and refrigerate.

Put the onion, chorizo, mushrooms and red pepper in the slow cooker pot. Add the garlic, rosemary, tomato purée and sugar, then stir in the sliced squid.

Pour the tomatoes and wine into a saucepan and bring to the boil; alternatively, heat in a microwave if you prefer. Add a little salt and pepper, then pour the mixture into the slow cooker pot and stir all ingredients together. Cover with the lid and cook on low for 3–5 hours or until the squid is tender.

When almost ready to serve, mix the cornflour to a paste with a little water in a small bowl. Stir into the slow cooker pot, add the squid tentacles, then replace the lid and cook on low for 30 minutes. Spoon the squid mixture into bowls lined with rice and serve sprinkled with chopped parsley, or serve with thickly sliced bread instead.

Prune Stuffed Pork Tenderloin

This is a great centrepiece for a special occasion, and is especially good accompanied with steamed asparagus or green beans and creamy potato dauphinoise.

Serves 4
Preparation time 40 minutes
Cooking temperature high
Cooking time 3½ –4 hours

2 pork tenderloins, just under
    400 g (13 oz) each
1 slice of bread, crusts
    removed
1 small onion, quartered
2 garlic cloves, halved
3.5 cm (1½ inch) piece of
    fresh root ginger, peeled and
    sliced
¼ teaspoon ground allspice
10 ready-to-eat pitted prunes
4 smoked streaky bacon
    rashers
1 tablespoon olive oil
12 shallots, halved if large
2 tablespoons cornflour
200 ml (7 fl oz) red wine
300 ml (½ pint) chicken stock
1 tablespoon tomato purée
salt and pepper

Preheat the slow cooker if necessary. Trim the thinnest end off each pork tenderloin so that each is 23 cm (9 inches) long, reserving the trimmings. Make a slit along the length of each and open out flat.

Put the pork trimmings into a food processor with the bread, onion, garlic, ginger, allspice and salt and pepper and mix until finely chopped. Spoon half the mixture along the length of 1 piece of pork, press the prunes on top, then cover with the rest of the stuffing and the remaining tenderloin. Season, then wrap the bacon around the pork and tie in place with string.

Heat the oil in a large frying pan, add the pork and shallots and fry, turning the pork, until golden all over. Transfer to the slow cooker pot. Make a smooth paste with the cornflour and a little cold water, then add to the pan with the remaining ingredients. Bring to the boil, stirring until thickened, then pour over the pork.

Cover with the lid and cook on high for 3½–4 hours or until the pork is cooked through and tender. Transfer the pork to a serving plate. Serve cut into thick slices, with the shallots and sauce.

For apricot & pistachio stuffed pork tenderloin, slit the tenderloins as above. Replace the prunes with 25 g (1 oz) roughly chopped pistachio nuts, the grated rind of ½ orange and 75 g (3 oz) chopped ready-to-eat dried apricots and add to the pork trimmings mixture, then continue as above. To make the sauce, replace the red wine with 200 ml (7 fl oz) dry cider.

Pulled Pork

Pulled pork originated in the Deep South of the United States but is popular the world round. This slow cooker version is a doddle to make and produces super-succulent results.

Serves 4
Preparation time 15 minutes
Cooking temperature high
Cooking time 5–6 hours

700 g (1 lb 6 oz) boneless pork
    shoulder joint, trimmed of fat
1 tablespoon treacle
½ teaspoon ground allspice
½ teaspoon ground ginger
½ teaspoon ground cumin
½ teaspoon crushed dried red
    chillies
¼ teaspoon salt
leaves from 2–3 thyme sprigs
1 onion, sliced
200 ml (7 fl oz) hot chicken
    stock
pepper

To serve
4 hamburger buns, split
4 lettuce leaves, shredded
3 tomatoes, thinly sliced
1 dill cucumber, drained and
    sliced

Preheat the slow cooker if necessary. Remove the strings, unroll the pork joint and make a cut through the middle to reduce the thickness by half. Place in the slow cooker pot and spread with the treacle.

Mix the ground spices, chillies, salt and thyme leaves together and season with pepper. Rub over the pork joint, then tuck the onion slices around it. Pour the hot stock over the onions, then cover with the lid and cook on high for 5–6 hours or until the pork is very tender.

Place the pork on a chopping board and pull into shreds using 2 forks. Top the bottom halves of the buns with the lettuce, tomato and dill cucumber, then pile the hot pork on top. Add a few of the onion slices to each bun and drizzle with the cooking juices. Replace the tops of the buns and serve.

For herby pulled pork, follow the recipe above to prepare the pork and spread it with the treacle. Mix the crushed dried red chillies, salt and thyme leaves with 2 finely chopped sage sprigs and rub over the treacle-spread pork. Add the onion and stock and continue as above.

Pot Roast Lamb with Za'atar Rub

A popular Middle Eastern spice blend, fragrant za'atar includes toasted sesame seeds, sumac – a dried berry with a tart lemony flavour – salt and other spices. It's a great match for the lamb in this recipe.

Serves 4
Preparation time 20 minutes
Cooking temperature high
Cooking time 5–6 hours

1 tablespoon extra virgin olive oil

2 onions, thinly sliced

2 garlic cloves, finely chopped

250 ml (8 fl oz) lamb stock

1 tablespoon tomato purée

2 teaspoons za'atar spice mix

200 ml (7 fl oz) dry white wine or extra lamb stock

1 tablespoon cornflour

400 g (13 oz) new potatoes, scrubbed and thickly sliced

½ boneless lamb shoulder, about 750 g (1½ lb)

salt and pepper

chopped parsley and mint, to garnish

To serve

2 courgettes, thinly sliced

1 tablespoon olive oil

½ teaspoon za'atar spice mix

400 g (13 oz) hummus

Preheat the slow cooker if necessary. Heat the oil in a large frying pan, add the onions and fry for 5 minutes until softened and just beginning to brown. Stir in the garlic, stock, tomato purée and half the za'atar. Pour in the wine or extra stock, reserving about 2 tablespoons.

Stir the cornflour into the reserved wine or stock until smooth, then add to the frying pan. Bring to the boil, stirring.

Add the potatoes to the base of the slow cooker pot, then pour in the hot stock mixture. Remove the strings from the lamb, open it out flat and rub with the reserved za'atar, then season with salt and pepper. Add to the slow cooker pot and press the meat beneath the liquid. Cover with the lid and cook on high for 5–6 hours or until the lamb is almost falling apart.

When almost ready to serve, toss the sliced courgettes with the oil, za'atar and a little salt and pepper. Cook in a preheated ridged griddle pan until lightly browned and tender. Divide the hummus between 4 serving plates, spread into an even layer and make a thin ridge around the sides to contain the lamb sauce. Break the lamb into pieces, then spoon it on to the hummus with the sauce. Add the courgettes and sprinkle with chopped parsley and mint.

For pot roast lamb with rosemary, add 200 ml (7 fl oz) red wine in place of the white wine, if using, in the sauce, plus 2 tablespoons redcurrant jelly and 3 rosemary sprigs. Mix the cornflour with the reserved wine or stock as above. Add the potatoes and plain lamb joint to the slow cooker, then pour over the hot stock mixture. Cook as above and serve with mixed steamed vegetables.

Slow-cooked Lamb Shanks

Lamb shanks get a North African spin, cooked with honey, olives and preserved lemons, in this lovely recipe.

Serves 4
Preparation time 20 minutes
Cooking temperature high
Cooking time 5–7 hours

2 tablespoons olive oil

4 lamb shanks, about 375 g
   (12 oz) each

625 g (1¼ lb) new potatoes,
   thickly sliced

2 onions, sliced

3–4 garlic cloves, finely
   chopped

300 ml (½ pint) white wine

150 ml (¼ pint) lamb stock

1 tablespoon runny honey

1 teaspoon dried oregano

75 g (3 oz) preserved lemons,
   cut into chunks

75 g (3 oz) green olives
   (optional)

salt and pepper

chopped parsley, to garnish

Preheat the slow cooker if necessary. Heat the oil in a large frying pan, add the lamb and fry, turning until browned on all sides. Arrange the potatoes in the base of the slow cooker pot, then put the lamb on top.

Add the onion to the pan and fry until softened, then mix in the garlic. Add the wine, stock, honey, oregano and a little salt and pepper and bring to the boil. Pour over the lamb, then add the lemons and olives, if using.

Cover with the lid and cook on high for 5–7 hours or until the potatoes are tender and the lamb is almost falling off the bone. Spoon into shallow bowls and sprinkle with parsley. Serve with a green salad.

For slow-cooked lamb shanks with prunes, fry the lamb as above and add to the potatoes. Fry the onion and garlic with 3 diced streaky bacon rashers, then mix in 300 ml (½ pint) red wine, 150 ml (¼ pint) lamb stock, 1 tablespoon tomato purée, 75 g (3 oz) pitted prunes, a small bunch of mixed herbs and salt and pepper. Cover and cook as above.

Moussaka

The classic version of this much-loved Greek dish is topped with a béchamel sauce, but this recipe has a quick and clever alternative, simply mixing yogurt, eggs and feta to create a creamy and delicious topping.

Serves 4
Preparation time 30 minutes
Cooking temperature low
Cooking time 8¾–11¼ hours

4 tablespoons olive oil
1 large aubergine, thinly sliced
500 g (1 lb) minced lamb
1 onion, chopped
2 garlic cloves, finely chopped
1 tablespoon plain flour
400 g (13 oz) can chopped
    tomatoes
200 ml (7 fl oz) lamb stock
1 teaspoon ground cinnamon
¼ teaspoon grated nutmeg
1 tablespoon tomato purée
salt and pepper

For the topping
3 eggs
250 ml (8 fl oz) natural yogurt
75 g (3 oz) feta cheese, grated
pinch of grated nutmeg

Preheat the slow cooker if necessary. Heat half the oil in a frying pan and fry the aubergine slices in batches, adding more oil as needed until they have all been fried and are softened and lightly browned on both sides. Drain and transfer to a plate.

Add the minced lamb and onion to the frying pan and dry fry, stirring and breaking up the lamb with a wooden spoon, until evenly browned. Stir in the garlic and flour, then mix in the tomatoes, stock, spices, tomato purée and a little salt and pepper. Bring to the boil, stirring.

Spoon the lamb mixture into the slow cooker pot and arrange the aubergine slices on top, overlapping. Cover with the lid and cook on low for 8–10 hours.

Make the custard topping. Mix together the eggs, yogurt, feta and nutmeg and spoon over the top of the aubergine. Replace the lid and cook, still on low, for ¾–1¼ hours or until set. Lift the pot out of the slow cooker using oven gloves and brown under a preheated hot grill. Serve with salad.

For Greek shepherd's pie, prepare the mince, top with the fried aubergine slices and cook as above. Omit the custard topping and instead cut 750 g (1½ lb) potatoes into chunks and cook in a saucepan of boiling water for 15 minutes or until soft. Drain and mash with 3 tablespoons Greek yogurt and some salt and pepper. Lift the pot out of the slow cooker using oven gloves, spoon the mash over the aubergine, dot with 25 g (1 oz) butter and brown under a preheated hot grill.

Pot Roast Lamb with Rosemary

(DF)

Serves 4
Preparation time 5 minutes
Cooking temperature high
Cooking time 7–8 hours

1–1.2 kg (2–2 lb 7 oz) half
    lamb shoulder on the bone
3 sprigs of rosemary
1 red onion, cut into wedges
2 tablespoons redcurrant jelly
250 ml (8 fl oz) red wine
250 ml (8 fl oz) lamb stock
salt and pepper

Slow cooked but super-speedy to prep, this oh-so-easy dish has deliciously rich and tender lamb that you can almost cut with spoon.

Preheat the slow cooker if necessary. Put the lamb into the slow cooker pot, add the rosemary on top and tuck the onion wedges around the sides of the joint.

Spoon the redcurrant jelly into a small saucepan and add the wine, stock and a little salt and pepper. Bring to the boil, stirring so that the jelly melts, then pour over the lamb. Cover with the lid and cook on high for 7–8 hours or until a knife goes into the centre of the lamb easily and the meat is almost falling off the bone.

Lift the joint out of the slow cooker pot and put it on to a serving plate with the onions. Discard the rosemary sprigs and pour the wine and stock mixture into a jug to serve as gravy. Carve the lamb on to plates and serve with steamed green vegetables and baby potatoes or Crushed New Potatoes with Rosemary Cream (see below).

For crushed new potatoes with rosemary cream, to serve as an accompaniment, bring a pan of water to the boil, add 500 g (1 lb) baby new potatoes and cook for 15 minutes. Add 200 g (7 oz) Tenderstem broccoli, thickly sliced, for the last 5 minutes. Drain and then roughly break up with a fork. Stir in 1 tablespoon finely chopped rosemary, 4 tablespoons crème fraîche and a little salt and pepper. Spoon a mound of potatoes into the centre of 4 serving plates, then top with the carved pot roast lamb and drizzle the gravy around the edges of the mash.

Turkey & Cranberry Meatloaf

This recipe delivers all the flavours of Christmas dinner in a meatloaf! Keep the Christmas theme going by serving it with steamed greens, roast parsnips and lots of cranberry sauce.

Serves 4–6
Preparation time 30 minutes, plus overnight chilling
Cooking temperature high
Cooking time 5–6 hours

1 tablespoon sunflower oil, plus extra for greasing
200 g (7 oz) smoked streaky bacon rashers
115 g (3¾ oz) pack dried orange and cranberry stuffing mix
25 g (1 oz) dried cranberries
1 onion, finely chopped
500 g (1 lb) skinless turkey breast steaks
1 egg, beaten
salt and pepper

Preheat the slow cooker if necessary. Lightly oil a soufflé dish, 14 cm (5½ inches) in diameter and 9 cm (3½ inches) high, and base-line with non-stick baking paper, checking first that the dish will fit in the slow cooker pot.

Stretch each bacon rasher with the flat of a large cook's knife, until half as long again, and use about three-quarters of the rashers to line the base and sides of the dish, trimming to fit.

Put the stuffing mix in a bowl, add the cranberries and mix with boiling water according to the pack instructions. Heat the oil in a frying pan, add the onion and fry for 5 minutes, stirring, until softened. Set aside. Finely chop the turkey slices in a food processor or pass through a coarse mincer.

Mix the stuffing with the fried onion, chopped turkey and egg. Season well and spoon into the bacon-lined dish. Press flat and cover with the remaining bacon rashers. Cover the top of the dish with foil and lower into the slow cooker pot.

Pour boiling water into the pot to come halfway up the sides of the dish. Cover with the lid and cook on high for 5–6 hours or until the juices run clear when the centre of the meatloaf is pierced with a knife.

Lift the dish out of the slow cooker pot using a tea towel and leave to cool. Transfer to the refrigerator to chill overnight until firm. Loosen the edge of the meatloaf with a knife, turn out on to a plate and peel off the lining paper. Cut into thick slices and serve with steamed greens, Roast Parsnips with Thyme Butter (see below) and spoonfuls of cranberry sauce.

For roast parsnips with thyme butter, toss 625 g (1¼ lb) scrubbed baby parsnips with 1 tablespoon extra virgin olive oil, 1 garlic clove, crushed, 2 thyme sprigs, chopped, 1 teaspoon grated lemon rind and a pinch each of cayenne pepper and sea salt in a roasting tin. Bake in a preheated oven, 200°C (400°F), Gas Mark 6, for 40–45 minutes, turning occasionally, until golden and tender. Serve at once.

Festive Nut Roast

This nut roast is so good, it will have the meat eaters around the table trying to get a look in. It also keeps really well in an airtight container or covered in foil in the refrigerator for up to 3 days.

Serves 6–8
Preparation time 1 hour
Cooking temperature high
Cooking time 4 hours

1 parsnip, peeled and cubed

1 carrot, peeled and cubed

2 tablespoons olive oil

1 red onion, finely chopped

2 garlic cloves, finely chopped

1 rosemary sprig, leaves
   picked and finely chopped

2 thyme sprigs, leaves picked

2 sage sprigs, leaves picked
   and finely chopped

2 tablespoons chopped flat leaf
   parsley, plus extra to garnish

½ teaspoon ground allspice

½ teaspoon ground nutmeg

180 g (6 oz) cooked chestnuts,
   roughly chopped

200 g (7 oz) mushrooms, finely
   chopped

300 g (10 oz) mixed nuts,
   toasted and roughly chopped

100 ml (3½ fl oz) hot stock

100 g (3½ oz) fresh
   breadcrumbs

100 g (3½ oz) dried
   cranberries

Preheat the slow cooker if necessary. Line the bottom and sides of a silicone or metal 900 g (2 lb) loaf tin with non-stick baking paper and grease with cooking spray or vegan butter. Ensure that the tin fits snugly (use some balls of foil to secure it if it doesn't quite reach the cooker bottom). Pour in enough water to come 2 cm (¾ inch) up the sides of the pot.

Cook the parsnip and carrot in a large saucepan of salted boiling water for about 10 minutes. Drain and leave to steam for 5 minutes. Transfer to a bowl and mash with a fork.

Heat the oil in a large frying pan over a medium heat, sauté the onion for 8–10 minutes until translucent. Add the garlic and cook for a further minute. Stir in the herbs and spices and cook for 2 minutes until fragrant. Add the chestnuts, mushrooms and nuts and cook for 5–8 minutes until the mushrooms have released all their moisture and the pan looks a little dry. Stir in the remaining ingredients and cook for 2–3 minutes until the stock has been absorbed.

Take the pan off the heat, stir through the parsnip and carrot and season to taste. Transfer the mixture to the prepared loaf tin, using the back of a spatula or spoon to push it down and make sure it is evenly spread. Place a tea towel or kitchen paper underneath the slow cooker lid, cover the cooker and cook on high for 4 hours until the nut roast is firm to the touch and no wet patches are visible.

Turn out of the tin and serve immediately, sprinkled with plenty of extra chopped parsley, and with Herb-roasted New Potatoes (see below) alongside.

For herb-roasted new potatoes, to serve as an accompaniment, put 2 tablespoons olive oil in a roasting tin and place in a preheated oven, 200°C (400°F), Gas Mark 6, for 5 minutes until hot. Add 1 kg (2 lb) scrubbed new potatoes, 4 peeled but whole garlic cloves, 2 rosemary sprigs, 2 thyme sprig, 1 sage spring. Season well with sea salt and pepper and turn to coat in the oil. Return to the oven and roast for 40–45 minutes, turning occasionally, until the potatoes are crisp and tender. Serve immediately.

Bacon & Leek Suet Pudding

Sometimes when it's grey and wet only a good old-fashioned meal hits the spot. This rib-sticking farmhouse classic is served with creamy parsley sauce.

Serves 4
Preparation time 30 minutes
Cooking temperature high
Cooking time 4–5 hours

25 g (1 oz) butter
2 smoked gammon steaks, about 450 g (14½ oz) in total, diced and any fat and rind discarded
250 g (8 oz) leeks, trimmed and sliced
300 g (10 oz) self-raising flour
150 g (5 oz) vegetable suet
3 teaspoons dry mustard powder
200–250 ml (7–8 fl oz) water
salt and pepper

For the parsley sauce
25 g (1 oz) butter
25 g (1 oz) plain flour
300 ml (½ pint) milk
20 g (¾ oz) parsley, finely chopped

Preheat the slow cooker if necessary. Heat the butter in a frying pan, add the gammon and leeks and fry, stirring, for 4–5 minutes or until the leeks have just softened. Season with pepper only. Leave to cool slightly.

Put the flour, ½ teaspoon salt, a large pinch of pepper, the suet and mustard powder in a bowl and mix well. Gradually stir in enough water to make a soft but not sticky dough. Knead lightly, then roll out on a large piece of floured non-stick baking paper to a rectangle 23 x 30 cm (9 x 12 inches). Turn the paper so that the shorter edges are facing you.

Spoon the gammon mixture over the pastry, leaving 2 cm (¾ inch) around the edges. Roll up, starting at the shorter edge, using the paper to help. Wrap in the paper, then in a sheet of foil. Twist the ends together tightly, leaving some space for the pudding to rise.

Transfer the pudding to the slow cooker pot and raise off the base slightly by standing it on 2 ramekin dishes. Pour boiling water into the pot to come a little up the sides of the pudding, being careful that the water cannot seep through any joins. Cover with the lid and cook on high for 4–5 hours or until the pudding is well risen.

Just before serving, melt the butter for the sauce in a saucepan. Stir in the flour, then gradually mix in the milk and bring to the boil, stirring until smooth. Cook for 1–2 minutes, then stir in the parsley and season. Lift the pudding out of the slow cooker pot, unwrap and cut into slices. Arrange on plates and spoon over a little sauce. Serve with sugar snap peas.

Venison Puff Pie

This pie rings the changes by using lean venison, in place of beef, and the juniper berries give a sharp, fruity note that really complements the meat.

Serves 4–5
Preparation time 35 minutes
Cooking temperature low
Cooking time 8–10 hours

25 g (1 oz) butter

1 tablespoon olive oil, plus extra for greasing

750 g (1½ lb) venison, diced

1 onion, chopped

2 tablespoons plain flour

200 ml (7 fl oz) red wine

250 ml (8 fl oz) lamb or beef stock

3 medium raw beetroot, peeled and cut into 1 cm (½ inch) dice

1 tablespoon redcurrant jelly

1 tablespoon tomato purée

10 juniper berries, roughly crushed

3 sprigs of thyme

1 bay leaf

1 sheet, about 200 g (7 oz), ready-rolled puff pastry

beaten egg, for glazing

salt and pepper

Preheat the slow cooker if necessary. Heat the butter and oil in a large frying pan, add the venison a few pieces at a time until all the pieces are in the pan, then fry, stirring, until evenly browned. Scoop the venison out of the pan with a slotted spoon and transfer to the slow cooker pot. Add the onion to the pan and fry for 5 minutes until softened.

Stir in the flour, then mix in the wine and stock. Add the beetroot, redcurrant jelly and tomato purée, then the juniper, 2 sprigs of thyme and the bay leaf. Season with salt and pepper and bring to the boil. Pour the sauce over the venison, cover with the lid and cook on low for 8–10 hours or until tender.

When you are almost ready to serve, preheat the oven to 220°C (425°F), Gas Mark 7. Unroll the pastry and trim the edges to make an oval similar in size to the slow cooker pot. Transfer to an oiled baking sheet, flute the edges and add leaves from the trimmings. Brush with egg, sprinkle with the remaining thyme leaves stripped from the stem and coarse salt and bake in the preheated oven for about 20 minutes until well risen and golden.

Stir the venison and spoon on to plates. Cut the pastry into wedges and place on top of the venison.

For lamb & mushroom puff pie, replace the venison with 750 g (1½ lb) diced shoulder or leg of lamb and fry as above. Fry the onion, then add 250 g (8 oz) quartered cup mushrooms in place of the beetroot and fry for 2–3 minutes. Stir in the flour and continue as above.

Beef & Guinness Puff Pie

This hearty pie with its blue cheese-topped pastry is a true winter warmer and can be made ahead of time. Serve with green beans and curly kale to balance the flavours.

Serves 4–5
Preparation time 40 minutes
Cooking temperature low
Cooking time 8–10 hours

2 tablespoons sunflower oil,
    plus extra for greasing
750 g (1½ lb) lean stewing
    beef, cubed
1 onion, chopped
2 tablespoons plain flour, plus
    extra for dusting
300 ml (½ pint) Guinness
150 ml (¼ pint) beef stock
2 teaspoons hot horseradish
1 tablespoon tomato purée
1 bay leaf
200 g (7 oz) cup mushrooms,
    sliced
salt and pepper

Pastry
500 g (1 lb) puff pastry, thawed
    if frozen
beaten egg, to glaze
100 g (3½ oz) Stilton cheese
    (rind removed), crumbled

Preheat the slow cooker if necessary. Heat the oil in a large frying pan, add the meat a few pieces at a time until all the pieces are in the pan, then add the onion and fry over a medium heat, stirring until the meat is evenly browned.

Stir in the flour, then gradually mix in the Guinness and the stock. Stir in the horseradish, tomato purée and a little salt and pepper, then add the bay leaf and bring to the boil. Transfer to the slow cooker pot and press the meat below the surface of the liquid. Cover with the lid and cook on low for 8–10 hours or until the meat is cooked through and very tender.

When almost ready to serve, preheat the oven to 200°C (400°F), Gas Mark 6. Discard the bay leaf and divide the beef mixture between 4 pie dishes, each about 450 ml (¾ pint). Mix in the mushrooms, then brush the top edge of the dishes with a little egg. Cut the pastry into 4 and roll each piece out on a floured surface until a little larger than the dishes, then press on to the dishes. Trim off the excess pastry and crimp the edges. Mark diagonal lines on top and brush with beaten egg. Put on an oiled baking sheet and cook in the preheated oven for 30 minutes or until golden. Sprinkle with the Stilton and leave to melt for 1–2 minutes.

For beery beef hotpot, make up the meat base as above, omitting the mushrooms and adding 2 diced carrots. Spoon into the slow cooker pot, then cover with 700 g (1 lb 6 oz) thinly sliced potatoes, pressing them just below the stock. Cook as above. Dot 25 g (1 oz) butter over the potatoes, lift the pot out of the slow cooker using oven gloves and brown under a hot grill.

Mushroom Leek Thyme Pie

This pie filling is so intensely creamy and rich that you will hardly believe that it's dairy free. Most shop-bought pastry is now vegan, which makes this speedy dinner a breeze. The filling also works well as a stew, if you want to skip the extra step of cooking the pastry.

Serves 4–6
Preparation time 1 hour, plus soaking
Cooking temperature low
Cooking time 4–5 hours

2 tablespoons sunflower or vegetable oil

2 large leeks, trimmed and sliced

500 g (1 lb) button mushrooms, halved

4 garlic cloves, finely chopped

2 thyme sprigs, leaves picked, plus extra leaves to garnish

200 g (7 oz) cashew nuts, soaked in cold water overnight or in boiling water for 1 hour, then drained

500 ml (17 fl oz) hot vegan bouillon stock

2 tablespoons nutritional yeast

1 teaspoon miso paste

finely grated rind and juice of 1 unwaxed lemon

1 sheet of vegan puff pastry

1 tablespoon dairy-free milk, to glaze

salt and pepper

Preheat the slow cooker if necessary. Heat the oil in a large frying pan over a medium heat, add the leeks and mushrooms and sauté for 10 minutes until the leeks are softened and the mushrooms are beginning to colour. Stir in the garlic and thyme leaves and cook for a further minute, then transfer the mixture to the slow cooker.

Blitz the cashew nuts, hot stock, nutritional yeast, miso paste and lemon rind and juice in a food processor or blender until smooth and creamy. Pour over the leek and mushroom mixture and stir to combine. Season with pepper, and salt if needed. Cover with the lid and cook on low for 4–5 hours until the sauce has thickened and the mushrooms are very soft. Add a splash of water or dairy free milk if the mixture seems too stiff.

Preheat the oven to 190°C (375°F), Gas Mark 5. If your slow cooker pot is ovenproof, remove it from the cooker, top with the sheet of puff pastry, trim the excess around the edge and crimp to secure. Use a pastry brush to brush the pastry with the dairy-free milk to glaze and bake in the oven for 30–40 minutes until the pastry is golden brown. Alternatively, transfer the filling to an ovenproof dish, then top with the pastry, glaze and bake in the same way.

Serve immediately, sprinkled with the extra thyme leaves.

Root Vegetable Puff Pastry Pie

This comforting autumnal pie is brilliant for feeding the family. Mix and match the root vegetables with what you have: white potatoes, celeriac and turnip all work well.

Serves 4
Preparation time 30 minutes
Cooking temperature low
Cooking time 6 hours 10 minutes

1 red onion, chopped

2 carrots, chopped

2 parsnips, chopped

1 sweet potato, peeled and chopped

2 floury potatoes (such as Maris Piper), peeled and chopped

3 garlic cloves, crushed

1 tablespoon thyme leaves

2 tablespoons plain flour

750 ml (1¼ pints) vegetable stock

75 ml (3 fl oz) double cream

100 g (3½ oz) frozen peas

1 tablespoon wholegrain mustard

1 egg, beaten

1 sheet puff pastry

salt and pepper

Preheat the slow cooker if necessary. Put the chopped vegetables, garlic and thyme into the slow cooker, then sprinkle over the flour and season well with salt and pepper. Toss the vegetables until well coated in the flour. Pour in the stock and stir together until well combined and there are no lumps of flour. Cover with the lid and cook on low for 6 hours.

Stir in the cream, frozen peas and mustard, replace the lid and cook, still on low, for a further 10 minutes until the sauce is thickened and creamy and the vegetables are tender.

Preheat the oven to 200°C (400°F), Gas Mark 6. Carefully spoon the vegetable mixture into a 23 x 33 cm (9 x 13 inch) ovenproof dish. Brush a little of the beaten egg around the top edges of the dish, then drape over the pastry sheet, pressing the edges to seal. Trim off any excess pastry, then brush the top with the remaining beaten egg.

Bake in the oven for 10 minutes until the top is golden brown and puffed up. Serve with steamed greens.

Sausage Tagliatelle

This hearty and flavour-filled pasta dish is sure to become a family favourite. All it needs to go with it is a crisp green salad dressed with a lemony vinaigrette.

Serves 4
Preparation time 25 minutes
Cooking temperature low
Cooking time 8–10 hours

1 tablespoon sunflower oil

8 chilli or spicy sausages

1 onion, chopped

150 g (5 oz) cup mushrooms, sliced

2 garlic cloves, finely chopped

400 g (13 oz) can chopped tomatoes

150 ml (¼ pint) beef stock

250 g (8 oz) tagliatelle

salt and pepper

To serve

basil leaves

freshly grated Parmesan cheese (optional)

Preheat the slow cooker if necessary. Heat the oil in a large frying pan, add the sausages and fry, turning until browned but not cooked through. Transfer to the slow cooker pot with tongs.

Drain off the excess fat from the pan to leave 2 teaspoons, then add the onion and fry until softened. Mix in the mushrooms and garlic and fry for 1–2 minutes.

Stir in the chopped tomatoes, stock and a little salt and pepper and bring to the boil, stirring. Pour the mixture over the sausages, cover with the lid and cook on low for 8–10 hours or until cooked through.

When almost ready to serve, bring a large saucepan of water to the boil, add the tagliatelle and cook for 7–8 minutes or until just tender then drain. Lift the sausages out of the slow cooker pot and slice thickly, then return to the pot with the pasta and mix together. Sprinkle with torn basil leaves and grated Parmesan, if liked.

For chicken & chorizo tagliatelle, omit the sausages and fry 500 g (1 lb) diced boneless chicken thighs in 1 tablespoon olive oil until golden. Drain and transfer to the slow cooker pot. Continue as above, adding 100 g (3½ oz) diced chorizo sausage to the frying pan with the onions and replacing the beef stock with 150 ml (¼ pint) chicken stock.

Peasant Paella

Originating in Valencia, Spain, paella was originally a simple peasant dish. This colourful, low-fat version is very easy to prepare and really full of flavour.

Serves 4
Preparation time 20 minutes
Cooking temperature high
Cooking time 4½–5¾ hours

low-calorie cooking oil spray
500 g (1 lb) boneless, skinless chicken thighs, cubed
1 onion, chopped
60 g (2¼ oz) chorizo, sliced
2 garlic cloves, finely chopped
1 red pepper, cored, deseeded and diced
1 orange pepper, cored, deseeded and diced
2 celery sticks, diced
2 pinches of saffron threads
½ teaspoon dried Mediterranean herbs
750 ml (1¼ pints) hot chicken stock
175 g (6 oz) easy-cook brown long-grain rice
125 g (4 oz) frozen peas
salt and pepper
2 tablespoons chopped parsley, to garnish

Preheat the slow cooker if necessary. Spray a large frying pan with a little low-calorie cooking oil spray and place over a high heat until hot. Add the chicken a few pieces at a time until all the chicken is in the pan and cook for 5 minutes, stirring, until browned. Use a slotted spoon to transfer the chicken to the slow cooker pot.

Add the onion, chorizo and garlic to the pan and cook for 3–4 minutes, stirring, until the onion is beginning to colour. Add the peppers and celery, stir well, then transfer to the slow cooker pot. Mix the saffron and dried herbs with the hot stock, season to taste, then pour into the slow cooker pot and stir well. Cover and cook on high for 3–4 hours.

Place the rice in a sieve and rinse under cold running water, then drain and stir into the chicken mixture. Cover again and cook, still on high, for 1½–1¾ hours until the rice is tender. Stir in the peas and continue cooking for 15 minutes. Serve garnished with the chopped parsley.

For seafood paella, follow the recipe above to cook the paella, omitting the chicken. Thaw a 400 g (13 oz) packet of frozen mixed seafood and pat dry on kitchen paper. Spray a large frying pan with a little low-calorie cooking oil spray and place over a high heat until hot. Add the seafood and fry for 4–5 minutes until piping hot. Stir into the finished paella and garnish with the parsley.

Pot-roast Pheasant with Chestnuts

Slow cooking this game bird really brings out the flavours. Paired here with its classic partner, chestnuts, this makes a wonderful alternative to turkey on Christmas Day for two or three people.

Serves 2–3
Preparation time 15 minutes
Cooking temperature high
Cooking time 3–4 hours

25 g (1 oz) butter

1 tablespoon olive oil

750 g (1½ lb) oven-ready
   pheasant

200 g (7 oz) shallots, halved

50 g (2 oz) smoked streaky
   bacon rashers, diced, or
   ready-diced pancetta

2 celery sticks, thickly sliced

1 tablespoon plain flour

300 ml (½ pint) chicken stock

4 tablespoons dry sherry

100 g (3½ oz) vacuum-packed
   prepared chestnuts

2–3 thyme sprigs

salt and pepper

Preheat the slow cooker if necessary. Heat the butter and oil in a frying pan, add the pheasant, breast side down, the shallots, bacon or pancetta and celery and fry until golden brown, turning the pheasant and stirring the other ingredients.

Transfer the pheasant to the slow cooker pot, placing it breast side down. Stir the flour into the onion mixture. Gradually add the stock and sherry, then add the chestnuts, thyme and a little salt and pepper. Bring to the boil, stirring, then spoon over the pheasant.

Cover with the lid and cook on high for 3–4 hours until tender. Test with a knife through the thickest part of the pheasant leg and breast to make sure that the juices run clear. Carve the pheasant breast into thick slices and cut the legs away from the body.

For pot-roast guinea fowl with prunes, fry a 1 kg (2 lb) guinea fowl instead of the pheasant as above. Transfer the fowl to the slow cooker, mix in 2 tablespoons plain flour, then add 450 ml (¾ pint) chicken stock and the sherry. Omit the chestnuts and add 75 g (3 oz) halved ready-to-eat pitted prunes instead. Continue as above, but cook for 5–6 hours.

Beetroot & Caraway Risotto

Caraway seeds give this vividly coloured risotto an earthy hint of mild aniseed. It's a great option for when you are really busy as you simply add all the ingredients to the slow cooker and give them a quick stir.

Serves 4
Preparation time 15 minutes
Cooking temperature low
Cooking time 5–6 hours

200 g (7 oz) long-grain
   brown rice
300 g (10 oz) beetroot, diced
1 red onion, finely chopped
2 garlic cloves, finely chopped
1 teaspoon caraway seeds
2 teaspoons tomato purée
1.2 litres (2 pints) hot
   vegetable stock
salt and pepper

To serve
4 tablespoons Greek yogurt
125 g (4 oz) smoked salmon
   slices
handful of rocket leaves

Preheat the slow cooker if necessary. Place the rice in a sieve, rinse well under cold running water and drain well.

Place the beetroot, onion and garlic in the slow cooker pot, add the drained rice, caraway seeds and tomato purée, then stir in the hot stock and season generously. Cover and cook on low for 5–6 hours until the rice and beetroot are tender.

Stir the risotto, spoon on to plates and top each portion with a spoonful of yogurt, some smoked salmon and a few rocket leaves. Serve immediately.

For pumpkin & sage risotto, place 300 g (10 oz) diced pumpkin in the slow cooker pot with 1 finely chopped white onion and 2 chopped garlic cloves. Mix in 250 g (8 oz) rinsed brown rice and flavour with 2 sage sprigs, 1 teaspoon paprika and 2 teaspoons tomato purée. Add 1.2 litres (2 pints) hot vegetable stock, season and cook as above. Serve sprinkled with 75 g (3 oz) finely grated Parmesan cheese.

Fish Terrine

This is a first course with serious wow factor. Light as a feather, it can also be served as part of buffet for a crowd.

Serves 6–8
Preparation time 30 minutes, plus cooling
Cooking temperature high
Cooking time 3–4 hours

375 g (12 oz) boneless
   haddock or cod loin, cubed
2 egg whites
grated rind of ½ lemon
juice of 1 lemon
250 ml (8 fl oz) double cream
125 g (4 oz) sliced smoked
   salmon or trout
150 g (5 oz) salmon or trout
   fillet, thinly sliced
salt and pepper

Preheat the slow cooker if necessary. Lightly oil a 1 litre (1¾ pint) soufflé dish and base-line with a circle of non-stick baking paper, checking first that the dish will fit in the slow cooker pot. Blend the haddock or cod loin, egg whites, lemon rind, half the lemon juice and salt and pepper in a food processor until roughly chopped, then gradually add the cream and blend until just beginning to thicken.

Arrange half the smoked fish slices over the base of the dish. Spoon in half the fish mousse and spread it level. Mix the fish fillet with a little remaining lemon juice and some pepper, then arrange on top. Top with the remaining fish mousse, then the smoked fish slices.

Cover the top with foil and lower into the slow cooker pot. Pour boiling water into the pot to come halfway up the sides of the dish. Cover with the lid and cook on high for 3–4 hours or until the fish is cooked through and the terrine is set.

Lift the dish out of the slow cooker pot using a tea towel and leave to cool for 2 hours. Loosen the edge, turn out on to a plate and peel off the lining paper. Cut into thick slices and serve with salad and toast.

For smoked haddock & chive terrine, make up the white fish mousse as above and flavour with 4 tablespoons chopped chives, 2 tablespoons chopped capers and the grated rind and juice of ½ lemon. Omit the smoked fish and arrange 1 sliced tomato over the base of the dish. Cover with half the fish mousse, 150 g (5 oz) thinly sliced smoked cod fillet, then the remaining fish mousse. Continue as above.

Duck, Pork & Apple Rillettes

This classic and decadent French dish of potted meats cooked slowly in their own fats makes a sensational starter.

Serves 4
Preparation time 30 minutes, plus cooling and overnight chilling
Cooking temperature high
Cooking time 5–6 hours

2 duck legs

500 g (1 lb) rindless belly pork rashers, halved

1 onion, cut into wedges

1 sharp dessert apple, such as Granny Smith, peeled, cored and thickly sliced

2–3 sprigs of thyme

250 ml (8 fl oz) chicken stock

150 ml (¼ pint) dry cider

salt and pepper

Preheat the slow cooker if necessary. Put the duck and belly pork into the base of the slow cooker pot. Tuck the onion and apple between the pieces of meat and add the thyme.

Pour the stock and cider into a saucepan and add plenty of salt and pepper. Bring to the boil, then pour into the slow cooker pot. Cover with the lid and cook on high for 5–6 hours or until the duck and pork are cooked through and tender.

Lift the meat out of the slow cooker pot with a slotted spoon and transfer to a large plate, then leave to cool for 30 minutes. Peel away the duck skin and remove the bones. Shred the meat into small pieces and discard the thyme sprigs. Scoop out the apple and onion with a slotted spoon, finely chop and mix with the meat, then taste and adjust the seasoning, if needed.

Pack the chopped meat mix into 4 individual dishes or small 'le parfait' jars and press down firmly. Spoon over the juices from the slow cooker pot to cover and seal the meat. Leave to cool, then transfer to the refrigerator and chill well.

When the fat has solidified on the top, cover each dish with a lid or clingfilm and store in the refrigerator for up to 1 week. Serve the rillettes with warm crusty bread, a few radishes and pickled shallots.

For chicken, pork & prune rillettes, omit the duck and put 2 chicken leg joints into the slow cooker pot with the belly pork rashers, onion and thyme, replacing the apple with 75 g (3 oz) ready-to-eat pitted prunes. Continue as above.

Tomato, Onion & Goats' Cheese Tart

A slow cooker acts as the perfect environment to confit tomatoes and garlic for this delicious tart. The confit mixture can be stored in the refrigerator and is also good served in salads or sandwiches.

Serves 6–8
Preparation time 45 minutes, plus cooling
Cooking temperature low
Cooking time 4 hours

500 g (1 lb) block shortcrust pastry
2 tablespoons olive oil
3 large onions, thinly sliced
1 tablespoon balsamic vinegar
2 tablespoons soft brown sugar
100 g (3½ oz) goats' cheese log with rind on, cut into thin slices
salt and pepper
thyme leaves, to garnish

For the confit tomatoes
1 kg (2 lb) mixed-colour cherry tomatoes
10 garlic cloves
a few rosemary and thyme sprigs
2 teaspoons sea salt
375 ml (13 fl oz) olive oil

Preheat the slow cooker if necessary. Put the cherry tomatoes, garlic, herbs, salt and oil into the slow cooker and mix together well. Cover with the lid and cook on low for 4 hours until the tomatoes are soft, tender and wrinkled. Carefully remove the slow cooker pot from the cooker using oven gloves and leave to cool (the confit mixture can be stored in an airtight container or sterilized jar in the refrigerator for up to 2 weeks).

Roll out the pastry on a lightly floured work surface, then use to line a 20 cm (8 inch) fluted tart tin. Chill in the refrigerator for 10 minutes. Preheat the oven to 180°C (350°F), Gas Mark 4. Line the case with baking paper, fill with baking beans and bake in the oven for 10 minutes. Remove from the oven and carefully lift out the paper and beans, then return to the oven and bake for a further 5 minutes until lightly golden and chalky to the touch. Leave to cool.

Meanwhile, heat the oil in a large frying pan, add the onions and a pinch of salt and fry over a low heat for about 15 minutes until very soft and golden brown. Stir in the vinegar and sugar and cook for a further 5 minutes until the onions are caramelized and all the liquid has been absorbed. Leave to cool slightly.

Increase the oven temperature to 200°C (400°F), Gas Mark 6. Spread a layer of the caramelized onions over the base of the baked pastry case. Using a slotted spoon, add a layer of the confit tomatoes, ensuring not to add too much oil. Top with the goats' cheese, drizzle with a little of the confit oil and season with pepper. Bake for 10 minutes until warmed through. Serve sprinkled with thyme leaves.

Mexican Stuffed Peppers

Serves 4–6
Preparation time 20 minutes
Cooking temperature low
Cooking time 6 hours

4–6 large peppers, any colour
    or a mixture
125 g (4 oz) quinoa
200 g (7 oz) can black beans,
    drained and rinsed
200 g (7 oz) can sweetcorn
    kernels, drained, or frozen
    and thawed
200 g (7 oz) passata
1 garlic clove, grated
1 tablespoon chipotle paste
2 teaspoons ground cumin
1 teaspoon sweet smoked
    paprika
salt and pepper

To serve
small handful of coriander
1 lime, cut into wedges

A stuffed pepper can feel a bit dated, but they're incredibly tasty and so simple to knock together that they deserve a spot back on our dinner tables. If peppers aren't your thing, try stuffing scooped-out large beef tomatoes or hollowed-out courgette halves instead.

Preheat the slow cooker if necessary. Slice the stalks and tops off the peppers and discard. Use a teaspoon or small serrated knife to remove the cores and seeds, taking care not to cut through the pepper flesh. Add 2 cm (¾ inch) of water to the slow cooker pot and arrange the peppers upright in the pot so that they fit snugly together.

Mix all the remaining ingredients together in a large bowl and season with salt and pepper. Spoon the filling evenly into the pepper shells, cover with the lid and cook on low for 6 hours until the quinoa is cooked through and the pepper shells have softened.

Serve immediately sprinkled with coriander leaves, along with Guacamole (see below) and lime wedges for squeezing over.

For guacamole, to serve as an accompaniment, halve and stone 3 ripe avocados, then scoop the flesh out of the shells into a bowl. Add 1 finely chopped tomato, a handful of finely chopped coriander leaves and ½ teaspoon ground cumin and roughly mash with a fork. Stir in a squeeze of lime juice and season to taste with salt. Serve immediately.

Sweet

Cinnamon Tahini Rolls

Banana & Walnut Bread

Zesty Marmalade Bread &
Butter Pudding

Sherried Bread & Butter
Puddings

Chocolate Croissant Pudding

Gingered Date &
Syrup Puddings

Syrup Sponge

Sticky Marmalade
Syrup Pudding

Jam Roly-Poly Pudding

Eve's Pudding

Mini Banana & Date Puddings

Topsy Turvy Plum Pudding

Cardamom Rice Pudding

Coconut Rice Pudding

Coconut & Rose Rice Pudding

Jamaican Ginger Cake

Dark Chocolate &
Armagnac Cake

Lemon & Poppy Seed
Drizzle Cake

Chocolate Lava Slab

Blueberry & Passion
Fruit Cheesecake

Chocolate & Espresso Mousse

Earl Grey Crème Brûlée

Peppermint & Raspberry Brûlée

Brandied Chocolate Fondue

Baked Honey &
Orange Custards

Chocolate & Coffee
Custard Creams

Plum & Blueberry Swirl

Hot Toddy Clementines

Raspberry & Rhubarb
Oaty Crumble

Cinnamon Tahini Rolls

These rolls take the fuss out of baking. You don't need to wait for the dough to rise, as the slow cooker does the job, so just put them in at night and wake up to gorgeous freshly cooked buns in the morning.

Makes 8–10 rolls
Preparation time 25 minutes, plus resting
Cooking temperature high
Cooking time 1½–2 hours

For the rolls
50 g (2 oz) vegan butter
2 tablespoons caster sugar
250 ml (8 fl oz) almond milk
7 g (about 2 teaspoons) fast-action dried yeast
400 g (13 oz) plain flour, plus extra for dusting
1 teaspoon sea salt

For the filling
75 g (3 oz) vegan butter
3 teaspoons ground cinnamon
1 teaspoon ground mixed spice
5 tablespoons light brown soft sugar
2 tablespoons tahini

For the icing
50 g (2 oz) icing sugar
3 tablespoons tahini
1–2 tablespoons almond milk

Melt the butter, sugar and almond milk and leave to cool. Stir in the yeast and leave to stand for about 5 minutes until it starts to foam.

Put the flour and salt into the bowl of a stand mixer fitted with a dough hook, add the yeast mixture and mix until a dough forms. Continue mixing on a low speed for 3–5 minutes until smooth and springy. Alternatively, mix the ingredients together with a wooden spoon in a large bowl, then turn out on to a lightly floured surface and knead by hand for 8–10 minutes until smooth and springy. Cover with a clean tea towel and leave to rest for 10–15 minutes.

Preheat the slow cooker if necessary. Meanwhile, mix together all the filling ingredients in a bowl.

Sprinkle the dough with a little flour and roll out on a lightly floured surface to about 30 x 40 cm (12 x 16 inches). Spread the filling over, right to the edges. Starting from a longer edge, roll the dough into a cylinder. Use a floured serrated knife to cut into 5 cm (2 inch) slices.

Line the bottom of the slow cooker with non-stick baking paper so that it comes at least 2 cm (¾ inch) up the sides. Place the rolls on their sides in the pot, spaced evenly apart. Place a tea towel or kitchen paper underneath the lid, cover and cook on high for 2 hours until the inner rolls are firm to the touch (check for doneness after 1½ hours and thereafter at frequent intervals until cooked).

Mix the icing ingredients to a spreadable consistency, adding more milk if necessary. Spread over the rolls while warm and serve immediately.

Banana & Walnut Bread

A classic banana and walnut bread recipe that is brilliant for afternoon tea or for breakfast. Cooking it in the slow cooker keeps the bread very moist and stops it from drying out.

Makes 10 slices
Preparation time 25 minutes
Cooking temperature high
Cooking time 2 hours

75 g (3 oz) unsalted butter, softened, plus extra for greasing
100 g (3½ oz) soft brown sugar
2 large eggs, lightly beaten
3 ripe bananas, mashed, plus 1 less ripe banana, halved lengthways, to decorate (optional)
1 teaspoon vanilla extract
225 g (7½ oz) plain flour
2 teaspoons baking powder
¼ teaspoon bicarbonate of soda
½ teaspoon fine salt
½ teaspoon ground cinnamon
½ teaspoon ground nutmeg
75 g (3 oz) walnuts, roughly chopped

Grease the bottom of a 900 g (2 lb) loaf tin. Cut a long strip of baking paper to fit the length and slightly above the short sides of the tin, then use it to line the tin (this makes it easier to remove the bread from the tin once baked).

Beat together the butter and sugar in a large bowl using a hand-held electric whisk until light and fluffy. Add the eggs, mashed bananas and vanilla extract and beat again until smooth and well combined.

Mix together the dry ingredients and two-thirds of the walnuts in a separate bowl, then fold into the banana mixture until the dry ingredients are well incorporated and there are no floury pockets.

Spoon the batter into the prepared loaf tin and smooth the top. Gently press the halved banana pieces, if using, into the batter, cut sides up, and sprinkle with the remaining walnuts.

Lower the tin into the slow cooker, then cover with the lid and cook on high for 2 hours, or until a metal skewer inserted into the middle of the bread comes out clean.

Carefully remove the tin from the slow cooker using oven gloves and leave the banana bread to cool in the tin. Remove using the baking paper tabs, then serve cut into slices.

Marmalade Bread & Butter Pudding

Serves 6
Preparation time 15 minutes
Cooking temperature high
Cooking time 2–2½ hours

50 g (2 oz) vegan butter, plus
    extra for greasing
6 thick slices of stale bread,
    sliced diagonally in half into
    triangles
3 tablespoons marmalade
1 unwaxed orange, thinly
    sliced
170 g (6 oz) silken tofu
250 ml (8 fl oz) dairy-free milk
115 g (4 oz) light brown soft
    sugar
1 teaspoon vanilla bean paste
finely grated rind of 1 unwaxed
    orange
icing sugar, for dusting

To make this a real showstopper, alternate slices of blood orange with the bread slices. This looks particularly stunning, and the rind cooks down until it is soft and delicious. This pudding feels like an incredibly indulgent breakfast for dessert.

Grease the slow cooker pot with vegan butter. Spread each triangle of bread with the vegan butter, on both sides, and spread the marmalade on one side of each. Arrange the bread slices in the slow cooker pot, cut edge down, so that they fit snugly together and look like mountain peaks. Nestle a slice of orange into each gap.

Blitz the tofu, dairy-free milk, brown sugar and vanilla bean paste in a food processor until smooth. Pour over the bread slices and sprinkle the orange rind on top.

Place a tea towel or kitchen paper underneath the slow cooker lid, cover the cooker and cook on high for 2–2½ hours until the bread has absorbed most of the liquid and the top is beginning to look a little golden.

Remove the slow cooker pot from the cooker, uncover and leave to cool slightly and firm up, then serve warm, dusted with icing sugar, along with dairy-free custard.

Sherried Bread & Butter Puddings

There's nothing quite so comforting as warm bread and butter pudding on a cold winter night. And it's even more soothing served with the Homemade Custard below.

Serves 4
Preparation time 20 minutes
Cooking temperature low
Cooking time 3½–4 hours

50 g (2 oz) mixed dried fruit

2 tablespoons sweet or dry
   sherry

1 tablespoon unsalted butter

100 g (3½ oz) white bread
   slices

6 teaspoons caster sugar

200 ml (7 fl oz) milk

1 teaspoon vanilla extract

2 eggs

Preheat the slow cooker if necessary. Place the dried fruit and sherry in a small saucepan and bring just to the boil. Remove from the heat and set aside.

Grease 4 x 200 ml (7 fl oz) heatproof dishes with a little butter, then use the rest to spread on the bread. Cut the bread into cubes, then layer in the dishes with the sherried fruit and 4 teaspoons of the sugar.

Beat the milk, vanilla and eggs in a jug, then strain into the dishes. Cover with squares of greased foil and stand in the slow cooker pot. Pour hot water into the pot to come halfway up the sides of the dishes, then cover and cook on low for 3½–4 hours or until the custard has set.

Sprinkle the tops of the puddings with the remaining sugar and brown with a cook's blow torch, or under a preheated hot grill. Serve warm with custard (see below for homemade).

For homemade custard, to serve with the puddings, beat 3 egg yolks with 3 tablespoons caster sugar and a few drops of vanilla extract in a bowl. In a saucepan, bring 300 ml (½ pint) milk just to the boil, then gradually mix into the egg mixture. Return to the pan and heat gently, stirring continuously, until the custard thickens and coats the back of a spoon (don't boil or the custard will curdle).

Chocolate Croissant Pudding

Don't let those stale chocolate croissants go to waste – use them to make this delectable pud instead. And for the chocoholics in your life, go one better and serve it with the rich hot Chocolate Sauce below.

Serves 4
Preparation time 15 minutes, plus soaking
Cooking temperature low
Cooking time 4–4½ hours

50 g (2 oz) butter

4 chocolate croissants

50 g (2 oz) caster sugar

¼ teaspoon ground cinnamon

40 g (1½ oz) pecan nuts, roughly crushed

300 ml (½ pint) milk

2 eggs

2 egg yolks

1 teaspoon vanilla extract

sifted icing sugar, to decorate

Butter the inside of a 1.2 litre (2 pint) straight-sided heatproof dish with a little of the butter, checking first that it will fit into the slow cooker pot.

Slice the chocolate croissants thickly and spread 1 side of each slice with the remaining butter. Mix together the caster sugar and cinnamon. Arrange the croissants in layers in the dish, sprinkling each layer with the spiced sugar and the pecans.

Whisk the milk, whole eggs, egg yolks and vanilla extract together in a mixing bowl. Pour into the dish and leave to soak for 15 minutes. Meanwhile, preheat the slow cooker if necessary.

Cover the top of the dish loosely with buttered foil and lower it into the slow cooker pot. Pour boiling water into the pot to come halfway up the sides of the dish, cover with the lid and cook on low for 4–4½ hours or until the custard is set and the pudding well risen. Lift the dish out of the slow cooker pot using a tea towel. Dust with sifted icing sugar. Scoop into bowls and serve with cream or Chocolate Sauce (see below).

For chocolate sauce, to serve as an accompaniment, melt 100 g (3½ oz) plain dark chocolate, chopped, 50 g (2 oz) unsalted butter, diced, and 1 tablespoon golden syrup in a saucepan over a low heat. Leave to cool slightly before serving.

Gingered Date & Syrup Puddings

Serves 4
Preparation time 20 minutes
Cooking temperature high
Cooking time 3½–4 hours

125 g (4 oz) pitted dates, chopped

125 ml (4 fl oz) boiling water

¼ teaspoon bicarbonate of soda

4 tablespoons golden syrup

50 g (2 oz) sunflower margarine, plus extra for greasing

50 g (2 oz) light muscovado sugar

100 g (3½ oz) self-raising flour

1 egg

1 teaspoon vanilla extract

1 teaspoon ground ginger

Who doesn't love an old-fashioned syrup pudding? These individual ginger-scented ones are lower in calories too so a great choice if you fancy a treat but are watching your weight.

Preheat the slow cooker if necessary. Place the chopped dates, measured boiling water and bicarbonate of soda in a bowl, stir and leave to soak for 10 minutes.

Meanwhile, lightly grease 4 metal pudding basins, each 200 ml (7 fl oz), and base-line with circles of non-stick baking paper. Divide the golden syrup between the basins.

Place the margarine, sugar, flour, egg, vanilla and ginger in a food processor and blend until smooth. Drain the dates, add to the processor and blend briefly to mix. Divide the mixture between the pudding basins, cover the tops with greased foil and put in the slow cooker pot.

Pour boiling water into the slow cooker pot to come halfway up the sides of the basins, cover and cook on high for 3½–4 hours until the sponge is well risen and springs back when pressed with a fingertip.

Lift the basins out of the pot using a tea towel. Remove the foil, loosen the edges of the puddings with a knife and turn out into shallow bowls. Peel away the lining paper and serve immediately with ice cream or frozen yogurt.

For gingered banana puddings, omit the dates, boiling water and bicarbonate of soda. Follow the recipe above, adding 1 ripe banana to the food processor with the remaining ingredients. Blend and continue as above.

Syrup Sponge

Incredibly nostalgic and easy, a slow cooker gives this classic pudding a moist and airy texture. You can also make individual sponges using 5 or 6 mini pudding tins or dariole moulds, following the same method but reducing the cooking time by an hour.

Serves 6–8
Preparation time 25 minutes, plus standing
Cooking temperature high
Cooking time 3–4 hours

85 g (3 oz) vegan butter, plus extra for greasing
75 g (3 oz) golden syrup
140 ml (4¾ fl oz) soya milk
½ tablespoon apple cider vinegar
85 g (3 oz) caster sugar
1 teaspoon vanilla bean paste
175 g (6 oz) self-raising flour
1 teaspoon baking powder
½ teaspoon salt
finely grated rind of 1 unwaxed lemon

Preheat the slow cooker if necessary. Grease a 1 litre (1¾ pint) pudding basin liberally with vegan butter, pour in the golden syrup and set aside. Mix together the soya milk and vinegar in a small bowl and leave to curdle for about 10 minutes.

Put the vegan butter, sugar and vanilla bean paste into the bowl of a stand mixer fitted with the whisk attachment, and whisk together until pale and fluffy, or whisk with a hand whisk in a bowl.

Mix together the remaining ingredients in a separate bowl. Fold into the sugar and butter mixture half at a time, alternating with the curdled soya milk half at a time, until all the ingredients are combined and no dry patches remain and you have a smooth batter.

Pour the batter into the pudding basin. Top a sheet of foil with a sheet of greased non-stick baking paper, fold together in a narrow pleat down the centre and place, greased side down, over the basin. Secure around the basin rim with a long length of string. Pass the string over the top of the basin and tie to the other side to create a handle. Put the pudding basin into the slow cooker. Pour in enough boiling water to come halfway up the sides. Cover with the lid and cook on high for 3–4 hours until a skewer inserted into the centre comes out clean.

Use the handle to lift the pudding basin out of the cooker, peel back the foil and paper and leave to stand for 5 minutes before turning out on to a plate to serve, with some dairy-free custard on the side.

Sticky Marmalade Syrup Pudding

This gloriously sticky pudding, with its gentle heat of ginger and tang of orange and marmalade, is almost impossible to resist.

Serves 4–5
Preparation time 20 minutes
Cooking temperature high
Cooking time 3–3½ hours

4 tablespoons golden syrup

3 tablespoons orange marmalade

175 g (6 oz) self-raising flour

75 g (3 oz) shredded vegetable suet

50 g (2 oz) light muscovado sugar

1 teaspoon ground ginger

grated rind and juice of 1 orange

2 eggs

2 tablespoons milk

Preheat the slow cooker if necessary. Lightly butter a 1.2 litre (2 pint) pudding basin and base-line with a circle of non-stick baking paper, checking first that it will fit in the slow cooker pot. Spoon the golden syrup and 2 tablespoons of the marmalade into the basin.

Put the flour, suet, sugar and ginger in a bowl and mix together. Add the remaining marmalade, orange rind and juice, the eggs and milk and beat until smooth. Spoon the mixture into the basin, spread it level and cover the top with buttered foil.

Lower the basin into the slow cooker pot and pour boiling water into the pot to come halfway up the sides of the basin. Cover with the lid and cook on high for 3–3½ hours or until the pudding is well risen and feels firm and dry when the top is pressed with a fingertip. Lift the basin out of the slow cooker pot using a tea towel and remove the foil. Loosen the edge of the pudding with a knife, turn out on to a plate and peel off the lining paper. Serve scoops of the pudding in bowls with custard or vanilla ice cream, if liked.

For sticky banana pudding, spoon 4 tablespoons golden syrup and 3 tablespoons light muscovado sugar into the base of the lined basin. Cut 2 bananas in half lengthways, then in half again crossways. Toss in the juice of ½ lemon and arrange, cut side down, in the bottom of the basin. Make up the pudding mixture, spoon over the bananas and continue as above.

Jam Roly-Poly Pudding

(V)

A childhood classic, jam roly-poly is proper comfort food, especially served with lots of hot custard. You can vary the jam filling – why not try the Blueberry Jam on page 12?

Serves 4
Preparation time 25 minutes
Cooking temperature high
Cooking time 3½–4 hours

300 g (10 oz) self-raising flour,
    plus extra for dusting
150 g (5 oz) shredded
    vegetable suet
50 g (2 oz) caster sugar
grated rind of 2 lemons
pinch of salt
200–250 ml (7–8 fl oz) milk or
    milk and water mixed
4 tablespoons strawberry jam

Preheat the slow cooker if necessary. Put the flour, suet, sugar, lemon rind and a pinch of salt in a bowl and mix well. Gradually stir in the milk or milk and water to make a soft but not sticky dough. Knead lightly, then roll out on a piece of floured non-stick baking paper to a rectangle about 23 x 30 cm (9 x 12 inches). Turn the paper so that the shorter edges are facing you.

Spread the jam over the pastry, leaving 2 cm (¾ inch) around the edges. Roll up, starting at a shorter edge, using the paper to help. Wrap in the paper, then in a sheet of foil. Twist the ends together tightly, leaving space for the pudding to rise.

Transfer the pudding to the slow cooker pot and raise off the base by standing it on 2 ramekin dishes. Pour boiling water into the pot to come a little up the sides of the pudding, being careful that the water cannot seep through any joins. Cover with the lid and cook on high for 3½–4 hours or until the pudding is light and fluffy. Lift out of the pot, then unwrap and cut into thick slices. Serve with hot custard.

For spotted dick, grate the rind of 1 large orange and reserve. Squeeze the juice into a saucepan, bring to the boil, add 150 g (5 oz) raisins and leave to soak for 30 minutes. Make up the pastry as above, adding the orange rind, the grated rind of 1 lemon and the soaked raisins before mixing with enough milk to make a soft dough. Shape into a log 23 cm (9 inches) long. Wrap in non-stick baking paper and foil, then cook as above.

Eve's Pudding

This old-fashioned favourite takes its name from the Bible story of Eve who tempts Adam with an apple. It's a delicious combination of apples and sponge that is equally good served with custard or vanilla ice cream.

Serves 4
Preparation time 25 minutes
Cooking temperature high
Cooking time 3–3½ hours

50 g (2 oz) unsalted butter, plus extra for greasing

50 g (2 oz) caster sugar

50 g (2 oz) self-raising flour

25 g (1 oz) ground almonds

¼ teaspoon baking powder

1 egg

grated rind and juice of 1 lemon

1 dessert apple, quartered, cored and sliced

1 tablespoon apricot jam

Preheat the slow cooker if necessary. Grease the base and sides of a 15 cm (6 inch) round ovenproof dish, about 6 cm (2½ inches) deep, with a little butter, checking first that it will fit in the slow cooker pot. Place the butter, sugar, flour, almonds and baking powder in a food processor, add the egg and lemon rind and blend until smooth. Spoon into the dish and spread level.

Toss the apple slices with the lemon juice, then overlap in a ring on top of the pudding mixture. Cover the dish with greased foil and put in the slow cooker pot. Pour boiling water into the slow cooker pot to come halfway up the sides of the dish, cover and cook on high for 3–3½ hours until a knife comes out cleanly when inserted into the centre.

Dot the top of the pudding with the apricot jam, then gently spread into an even layer. Place under a preheated hot grill for 3–4 minutes until the top is lightly caramelized. Serve with custard or ice cream.

For chocolate & pear pudding, follow the recipe above to make the pudding base, using 1 tablespoon cocoa powder instead of the lemon rind. Quarter, core and slice 1 small pear, toss with the lemon juice, then arrange over the pudding mixture. Cover and bake as above, then dust the top with a little sifted icing sugar before serving.

Mini Banana & Date Puddings

Drenched in toffee and chocolate sauce, these little banana-flavoured puds are a delight. For a boozy version, add a tablespoon of brandy to the mixture before cooking.

Serves 4
Preparation time 20 minutes
Cooking temperature high
Cooking time 2–3 hours

100 g (3½ oz) butter, at room temperature, plus extra for greasing

100 g (3½ oz) light muscovado sugar

2 eggs, beaten

125 g (4 oz) self-raising flour

1 small ripe banana, mashed

75 g (3 oz) ready-chopped stoned dates

250 g (8 oz) ready-made toffee sauce

50 g (2 oz) plain dark chocolate, broken into pieces

Preheat the slow cooker if necessary. Butter 4 metal pudding moulds, each 250 ml (8 fl oz), and base-line each with a circle of non-stick baking paper, checking first that they will fit in the slow cooker pot.

Beat the butter and sugar in a bowl with a wooden spoon or hand-held electric whisk until soft and creamy. Gradually add alternate spoonfuls of egg and flour until both have all been added and the mixture is smooth. Mash the banana on a plate, then beat into the pudding mix. Stir in the dates, then divide between the moulds.

Cover each one with a square of foil and stand in the slow cooker pot. Pour boiling water into the pot to come halfway up the sides of the moulds. Cover with the lid and cook on high for 2–3 hours or until the tops of the puddings spring back when pressed with a fingertip.

Lift the moulds from the slow cooker pot using a tea towel and remove the foil. Loosen the edges with a knife and turn out on to plates. Pour the toffee sauce into a small saucepan, add the chocolate and warm through, stirring until the chocolate has just melted. Drizzle over the puddings and serve immediately.

For mini chocolate & banana puddings, make up the puddings with the butter, sugar and eggs as above. Substitute 15 g (½ oz) cocoa for the same weight of flour, then add with the remaining flour, mashed banana and dates. Cook as above. Warm 4 tablespoons chocolate and hazelnut spread with 2 tablespoons double cream and 2 tablespoons milk in a saucepan, stir until smooth and serve with the puddings.

Topsy Turvy Plum Pudding

(V)

This upside-down sponge pudding captures all the flavours of autumn with it's sticky topping of stewed blackberries and plums.

Serves 6
Preparation time 25 minutes
Cooking temperature high
Cooking time 4–5 hours

100 g (3½ oz) butter, at room temperature, plus extra for greasing
100 g (3½ oz) blackberries, thawed if frozen
200 g (7 oz) ripe red plums, halved, stoned and sliced
2 tablespoons red berry jam
100 g (3½ oz) caster sugar
100 g (3½ oz) self-raising flour
2 eggs, beaten
50 g (2 oz) ground almonds
few drops of almond extract
toasted flaked almonds, to decorate (optional)

Preheat the slow cooker if necessary. Lightly butter a 1.2 litre (2 pint) soufflé dish and base-line with a circle of non-stick baking paper, checking first that the dish will fit in the slow cooker pot. Arrange the blackberries and plums in the base, then dot with the jam.

Beat the butter and sugar in a bowl with a wooden spoon or hand-held electric whisk until soft and creamy. Gradually mix in alternate spoonfuls of flour and beaten egg, and continue adding and beating until the mixture is smooth. Stir in the almonds and almond extract. Spoon the mixture over the fruit, spread it level and cover the top with foil.

Lower the dish into the slow cooker pot and pour boiling water into the pot to come halfway up the sides of the dish. Cover with the lid and cook on high for 4–5 hours or until the sponge is well risen and springs back when pressed with a fingertip.

Lift the dish out of the slow cooker pot using a tea towel and remove the foil. Loosen the edges of the pudding with a knife and turn out on to a plate with a rim. Decorate with toasted flaked almonds, if liked, and serve hot with custard.

For peach & chocolate pudding, arrange 2 (or 1 if very large) halved, stoned and sliced ripe peaches in the base of the dish and dot with 2 tablespoons apricot jam. Make up the sponge mixture as above, adding 25 g (1 oz) cocoa powder and an extra 25 g (1 oz) self-raising flour instead of the ground almonds and almond extract. Continue as above.

Cardamom Rice Pudding

This creamy rice pudding has a gentle aromatic flavour from the cardamom and is incredibly comforting. It is lovely served on its own or with the Speedy Apple Compote below.

Serves 6
Preparation time 5 minutes
Cooking temperature low
Cooking time 4 hours

5 cardamom pods

150 g (5 oz) pudding rice

1 litre (1¾ pints) milk or dairy-free milk, such as almond or oat

60 g (2¼ oz) demerara sugar

1 cinnamon stick

½ teaspoon ground nutmeg

½ teaspoon vanilla bean paste

Preheat the slow cooker if necessary. Crush the cardamom pods lightly using a pestle and mortar, then remove the skins. Crush the seeds to a fine powder, then transfer to the slow cooker.

Add the remaining ingredients, cover with the lid and cook on low for 4 hours until the rice is tender, creamy and most of the liquid has been absorbed. Remove the cinnamon stick before serving.

Serve warm with Speed Apple Compote (see below), if you like.

For speedy apple compote, to serve as an accompaniment, melt 50 g (2 oz) unsalted butter or margarine, if you want to keep it vegan, in a saucepan, then add 4 peeled, cored and chopped apples, 2 tablespoons caster sugar and ½ teaspoon ground cinnamon. Cook for about 5 minutes, stirring occasionally, until the apples have softened. Dollop over the rice pudding to serve.

Coconut Rice Pudding

 GF VE

Creamy, smooth and moreish, this rice pudding has such a silky finish thanks to the rich coconut milk. Serve with a dollop of jam for an old-school pudding. Alternatively, keep things tropical by sprinkling with desiccated coconut or serving with chopped mango, pineapple or banana.

Serves 6
Preparation time 5 minutes
Cooking temperature high
Cooking time 2–2½ hours

100 g (3½ oz) pudding rice
400 ml (14 fl oz) can coconut milk
400 ml (14 fl oz) unsweetened almond milk or soya milk
125 g (4 oz) light brown soft sugar
1 cinnamon stick

Preheat the slow cooker if necessary. Grease the slow cooker pot with non-stick cooking spray or vegan butter.

Put all the ingredients into the slow cooker, cover with the lid and cook on high for 2–2½ hours until the rice is very tender and the mixture has thickened but is still creamy. Discard the cinnamon stick and serve immediately.

For rice pudding with drunken raisins, put 75 g (2¾ oz) raisins in a saucepan with 3 tablespoons vegan sherry or Madeira and warm together over a low heat, or microwave the raisins and wine in a small bowl for 30 seconds on full power. Leave to soak for at least 30 minutes or longer if possible, then add to the slow cooker with all the ingredients above and follow the recipe above.

Coconut & Rose Rice Pudding

Redolent with the delicate floral aroma and taste of rosewater, this is a mouthwatering Middle Eastern-style spin on rice pudding.

Serves 4
Preparation time 10 minutes
Cooking temperature high
Cooking time 2½–3 hours

65 g (2½ oz) pudding rice, rinsed and drained

50 g (2 oz) caster sugar

25 g (1 oz) desiccated coconut, plus 2 teaspoons, to decorate

600 ml (1 pint) milk

½–1 teaspoon rosewater, to taste

125 g (4 oz) raspberries, to serve

Preheat the slow cooker if necessary. Place the rice, sugar and the 25 g (1 oz) coconut in the slow cooker pot, add the milk and stir well. Cover and cook on high for 2½–3 hours until the rice is tender.

Stir well, then add the rosewater. Spoon into bowls, top with the raspberries and the remaining 2 teaspoons coconut and serve immediately.

For vanilla & orange rice pudding, split 1 vanilla pod lengthways and scrape out the seeds with a small knife. Follow the recipe above, adding the vanilla seeds to the rice and milk in the slow cooker pot with the vanilla pod and the finely grated rind of ½ orange. Stir well, cover and cook as above. Stir again and remove the vanilla pod before serving with raspberries and a sprinkling of coconut.

Jamaican Ginger Cake

This cake is so soft and moist, and will keep in an airtight container for up to a week – perfect for unexpected visitors at teatime. And you can also serve it as a vegetarian dessert – simply add some vanilla ice cream and pour over the heavenly Chocolate & Ginger Sauce below.

Makes a 900 g (2 lb) loaf cake
Preparation time 20 minutes, plus cooling
Cooking temperature high
Cooking time 2–2½ hours

2 tablespoons ground flaxseed

4 tablespoons cold water

200 g (7 oz) plain flour

2 teaspoons bicarbonate of soda

1 tablespoon ground ginger

1 teaspoon ground mixed spice or allspice

½ teaspoon salt

85 g (3 oz) vegan butter

85 g (3 oz) black treacle

85 g (3 oz) golden syrup

85 g (3 oz) dark brown soft sugar

140 ml (4¾ fl oz) almond milk

25–50 g (1–2 oz) stem ginger in syrup, to taste, finely chopped

Preheat the slow cooker if necessary. Line the bottom and sides of a silicone or metal 900 g (2 lb) loaf tin with non-stick baking paper and grease with non-stick cooking spray or vegan butter. Ensure that the tin fits snugly inside the slow cooker pot, using some scrunched-up balls of foil to raise the tin slightly off the bottom, or to secure it if it doesn't quite reach the cooker bottom.

Mix the ground flaxseed with the measured cold water in a small bowl and leave to stand for about 5 minutes until thickened. Meanwhile, sift the flour, bicarbonate of soda, spices and salt into a bowl and set aside.

Heat the vegan butter, black treacle, golden syrup and sugar in a saucepan over a gentle heat until just melted, then remove from the heat and beat into the flour mixture. Add the flaxseed mixture and the almond milk and mix until smooth. Fold in the stem ginger.

Pour the batter into the prepared tin. Place a tea towel or kitchen paper underneath the lid, cover the cooker and cook on high for 2–2½ hours until a skewer inserted into the centre comes out clean.

Remove from the slow cooker and leave to cool in the tin for 10 minutes. Then use the lining paper to lift the cake out of the tin and leave to cool completely on a wire rack before serving.

For chocolate & ginger sauce, to serve as an accompaniment, melt together 200 g (7 oz) dark chocolate, broken into small pieces, 300 ml (½ pint) double cream, 2 pieces of stem ginger in syrup, finely chopped, and 2 tablespoons stem ginger syrup in a saucepan over a low heat. Cook until melted and smooth and shiny, stirring occasionally.

Dark Chocolate & Armagnac Cake

This rich and decadent cake calls for Armagnac-soaked prunes, which add a delicious boozy kick. The result is rich and chocolatey.

Serves 6
Preparation time 20 minutes, plus soaking
Cooking temperature high
Cooking time 1½ hours

200 g (7 oz) soft pitted prunes, roughly chopped

50 ml (2 fl oz) Armagnac

2 teaspoons vanilla extract

200 g (7 oz) plain dark chocolate, broken into pieces

100 g (3½ oz) unsalted butter, plus extra for greasing

4 large eggs

200 g (7 oz) caster sugar

½ teaspoon fine salt

100 g (3½ oz) ground almonds

50 g (2 oz) plain flour

cocoa powder, for dusting

Put the prunes into a shallow dish, then pour over the Armagnac and vanilla extract and leave to soak for a minimum of 2 hours or preferably overnight.

Preheat the slow cooker if necessary. Melt the chocolate and butter in a heatproof bowl set over a saucepan of gently simmering water, ensuring the bottom of the bowl does not touch the water. Remove from the heat and leave to cool slightly.

Grease a 20 cm (8 inch) springform cake tin with butter and line with baking paper. Seal around the outside bottom edge with foil.

Whisk together the eggs, sugar and salt in a large bowl until pale and fluffy, then carefully fold in the melted chocolate and soaked prunes, including the liquid. Fold in the ground almonds and flour, taking care not to overmix and knock the air out. Pour the batter into the prepared cake tin.

Lower the tin into the slow cooker, then carefully pour boiling water into the pot to come about halfway up the side of the tin. Cover with the lid and cook on high for 1½ hours until the cake is set but still has a slight wobble in the middle.

Carefully remove the tin from the slow cooker using oven gloves and transfer to a wire rack to cool the cake completely, then remove from the tin and serve cut into slices. Dust with cocoa powder and serve with crème fraîche.

Lemon & Poppy Seed Drizzle Cake

This light and zesty cake will be everyone's favourite. For maximum tang and flavour, pour the syrup over the hot cake as quick as you can so it soaks right in.

Serves 6–8
Preparation time 25 minutes, plus cooling and soaking
Cooking temperature high
Cooking time 4½–5 hours

125 g (4 oz) butter, at room temperature, plus extra for greasing
125 g (4 oz) caster sugar
125 g (4 oz) self-raising flour
2 eggs, beaten
2 tablespoons poppy seeds
grated rind of 1 lemon
lemon rind curls, to decorate

For the lemon syrup
juice of 1½ lemons
125 g (4 oz) caster sugar

Preheat the slow cooker if necessary. Lightly butter a soufflé dish 14 cm (5½ inches) in diameter and 9 cm (3½ inches) deep, and base-line with a circle of non-stick baking paper, checking first that it will fit in the slow cooker pot.

Cream together the butter and sugar in a mixing bowl with a wooden spoon or hand-held electric whisk until soft and creamy. Gradually mix in alternate spoonfuls of the flour and beaten egg, and continue adding and beating until the mixture is smooth. Stir in the poppy seeds and lemon rind, then spoon the mixture into the soufflé dish and spread the top level. Cover the top of the dish loosely with buttered foil and then lower into the slow cooker pot.

Pour boiling water into the slow cooker pot so that it comes halfway up the sides of the dish. Cover with the lid and cook on high for 4½–5 hours or until the cake is dry and springs back when pressed with a fingertip.

Lift the dish carefully out of the slow cooker using a tea towel, remove the foil and loosen the edge of the cake with a knife. Turn out on to a plate or shallow dish with a rim and remove the lining paper.

Quickly warm the lemon juice and sugar together for the syrup, and as soon as the sugar has dissolved, pour the syrup over the cake. Leave to cool and for the syrup to soak in. Cut into slices and serve with spoonfuls of crème fraîche, decorated with lemon rind curls.

For citrus drizzle cake, omit the lemon rind and poppy seeds from the cake mixture and stir in the grated rind of ½ lemon, ½ lime and ½ small orange. Bake as above. Make the syrup using the juice of the grated fruits and sugar as above.

Chocolate Lava Slab

(VE)

Any leftovers of this incredibly rich chocolate cake will keep well in the refrigerator, covered in foil, for up to 3 days. The sauce is absorbed into the cake slightly so it ends up tasting like a fudgy brownie – you could reheat it in the microwave before serving.

Serves 6–8
Preparation time 20 minutes, plus cooling
Cooking temperature low
Cooking time 3–4 hours

125 g (4 oz) plain flour

150 g (5 oz) caster sugar

3 tablespoons cocoa powder

2 teaspoons baking powder

½ teaspoon salt

125 ml (4 fl oz) dairy-free milk

75 ml (3 fl oz) sunflower or vegetable oil

1 teaspoon vanilla bean paste

150 g (5 oz) vegan dark chocolate chips (optional)

For the topping

150 g (5 oz) light brown soft sugar

3 tablespoons cocoa powder

350 ml (12 fl oz) freshly brewed hot coffee, or
    1 tablespoon instant coffee powder mixed with 350 ml (12 fl oz) boiling water

Preheat the slow cooker if necessary. Grease the slow cooker pot with vegan butter and line the bottom and sides with non-stick baking paper, or simply grease with non-stick cooking spray.

Mix together the dry ingredients in a large bowl until well combined. Add the dairy-free milk, oil and vanilla bean paste and whisk until combined, but take care not to overmix. Fold in the chocolate chips, if using, or reserve them for sprinkling over the batter.

Pour the batter into the slow cooker and spread it out evenly, then sprinkle over the chocolate chips, if using and not already added.

Mix together the brown sugar and cocoa powder in a jug, add the hot coffee and whisk to combine. Pour the hot sauce carefully over the cake batter (you can pour it over the back of a dessertspoon to make sure the flow of water doesn't disturb your batter) and leave it to sit on top, without stirring in. Cover with the lid and cook on low for 3–4 hours or until a skewer inserted into the top half of the cake comes out clean (don't be misled by the saucy layer on the bottom).

Remove the slow cooker pot from the cooker, uncover and leave the cake to cool and firm up for at least 15 minutes before serving.

Blueberry & Passion Fruit Cheesecake

Who doesn't love cheesecake? This low-cal cheesecake is topped with an irresistible combination of blueberries and sweetly sharp passion fruit.

Serves 4
Preparation time 25 minutes, plus cooling and chilling
Cooking temperature high
Cooking time 2–2½ hours

1 tablespoon sunflower margarine, plus extra for greasing

75 g (3 oz) reduced-fat digestive biscuits, finely crushed

300 g (10 oz) extra-light soft cheese

175 ml (6 fl oz) fat-free Greek yogurt

1 tablespoon cornflour

finely grated rind and juice of ½ lime

1 teaspoon vanilla extract

3 tablespoons granular sweetener

3 tablespoons caster sugar

2 eggs

125 g (4 oz) blueberries

2 passion fruit, halved

Preheat the slow cooker if necessary. Grease the base and sides of a 15 cm (6 inch) round ovenproof dish, about 6 cm (2½ inches) deep, with a little margarine. Line the base with non-stick baking paper.

Melt the margarine in a small saucepan and stir in the crushed biscuits. Spoon into the dish and press down firmly to make a thin, even layer. Place the cheese, yogurt and cornflour in a mixing bowl and whisk until smooth. Add the lime rind and juice, vanilla, sweetener, sugar and eggs and whisk again until smooth.

Pour the mixture into the dish and smooth the surface.

Cover with greased foil and put in the slow cooker pot. Pour boiling water into the slow cooker pot to come halfway up the sides of the dish, cover and cook on high for 2–2½ hours or until the cheesecake is set but with a slight wobble in the centre. Remove from the slow cooker and leave to cool, then chill in the refrigerator for 3–4 hours or overnight.

Loosen the edge of the cheesecake with a knife, turn out of the dish and peel away the lining paper. Place on a serving plate, pile the blueberries on top, then scoop the passion fruit seeds over them. Serve cut into wedges.

For summer berry cheesecake, follow the recipe above to make the cheesecake, using the grated rind and juice of ½ lemon instead of the lime. Gently toss 100 g (3½ oz) sliced strawberries and 100 g (3½ oz) raspberries with 2 tablespoons reduced-sugar strawberry jam and 1 tablespoon lemon juice instead of the blueberries and passion fruits. Turn out the cheesecake and top with the berry mixture just before serving.

Chocolate & Espresso Mousse

 (GF) (V)

Serves 4
Preparation time 25 minutes
Cooking temperature high
Cooking time 1 hour

150 g (5 oz) plain dark
  chocolate, broken into pieces
100 ml (3½ fl oz) freshly made
  strong espresso, cooled
pinch of sea salt
3 large eggs, separated
100 g (3½oz) caster sugar

To serve
chocolate shavings
handful of chopped pistachio
  nuts

These little chocolate mousses with an espresso hit are a real crowd-pleaser and look like they are far more work than they really are. The chopped pistachios on top give the mousse a lovely crunchy, nutty flavour. For a special occasion, top them with the boozy Mint Syllabub below.

Preheat the slow cooker if necessary. Melt the chocolate in a heatproof bowl set over a saucepan of gently simmering water, ensuring the bottom of the bowl does not touch the water. Remove from the heat and leave to cool slightly, then stir in the espresso and salt.

Whisk together the egg yolks and sugar in a separate bowl with a hand-held electric whisk until pale, fluffy and voluminous. Add the melted chocolate mixture and stir until combined.

Whisk the egg whites in a clean bowl using clean beaters until medium-soft peaks form, then gently fold into the chocolate mixture until combined. Spoon the mousse into 4 x 9 cm (3½ inch) ramekins.

Lower the ramekins into the slow cooker, then carefully pour boiling water into the pot to come about halfway up the sides of the dishes. Cover with the lid and cook on high for 1 hour until just set.

Carefully remove the ramekins from the slow cooker using a clean tea towel and leave to cool slightly. Serve topped with chocolate shavings and a sprinkle of pistachio nuts and Mint Syllabub (see below), if you like.

For mint syllabub, to serve as an accompaniment, place 75 ml (3 fl oz) crème de menthe liqueur, 25 g (1 oz) caster sugar, 1 tablespoon lime juice in a bowl and beat with a hand-held electric whisk, then whisk in 300 ml (½ pint) double cream until it forms soft peaks.

Earl Grey Crème Brûlée

A slow cooker is perfect for creating crème brûlée because the temperature is low and controlled, and creating a water bath cooks these Earl Grey-flavoured custards really gently.

Serves 2
Preparation time 20 minutes, plus standing and cooling
Cooking temperature low
Cooking time 2 hours

400 ml (14 fl oz) double cream
100 ml (3½ fl oz) milk
1 tablespoon vanilla bean paste
2 Earl Grey tea bags
3 large egg yolks
75 g (3 oz) caster sugar, plus 2 tablespoons for the crust

Preheat the slow cooker if necessary. Put the cream, milk, vanilla and tea bags into a saucepan and warm over a medium heat until just below boiling point, then remove from the heat, cover with a lid and leave to stand for 10 minutes.

Whisk together the egg yolks and sugar in a large heatproof bowl until pale and fluffy. Remove the teabags from the milk mixture, then slowly pour over the egg yolks, whisking continuously. Pour the mixture into 2 x 9 cm (3½ inch) ramekins.

Lower the ramekins into the slow cooker, then carefully pour boiling water into the pot to come about halfway up the sides of the dishes. Cover with the lid and cook on low for 2 hours until the custard is set.

Carefully remove the ramekins from the slow cooker using a clean tea towel and transfer to a wire rack to cool. When cool enough to handle, transfer to the refrigerator and leave to cool completely for 1–2 hours or chill overnight.

When ready to serve, sprinkle a tablespoon of sugar in an even layer over each ramekin, tapping off any excess. Heat the tops using a kitchen blowtorch until the sugar is crisp and caramelized. Alternatively, place the ramekins under a preheated hot grill for 2 minutes until caramelized. Leave the sugar to cool and harden for a couple of minutes before serving.

Peppermint & Raspberry Brûlée

This light and zesty cake will be everyone's favourite. For maximum tang and flavour, pour the syrup over the hot cake as quick as you can so it soaks right in.

Serves 4
Preparation time 30 minutes, plus chilling
Cooking temperature low
Cooking time 2½–3½ hours

4 egg yolks
40 g (1½ oz) caster sugar
400 ml (14 fl oz) double cream
¼ teaspoon peppermint extract
150 g (5 oz) raspberries
2 tablespoons icing sugar

Preheat the slow cooker if necessary. Whisk the egg yolks and sugar in a bowl for 3–4 minutes until frothy, then gradually whisk in the cream. Stir in the peppermint extract, then strain the egg custard into a jug.

Pour into 4 ramekin dishes, each 150 ml (¼ pint), checking first that they will fit in the slow cooker pot. Put the dishes into the slow cooker pot, pour boiling water into the pot to come halfway up the sides of the dishes, then loosely cover the top of each dish with foil.

Cover with the lid and cook on low for 2½–3½ hours or until the custard is set with a slight quiver to the middle. Lift the dishes carefully out of the slow cooker and leave to cool. Transfer to the refrigerator to chill for 4 hours.

When ready to serve, pile a few raspberries in the centre of each dish and sprinkle over some icing sugar. Caramelize the sugar with a cook's blow torch or under a preheated hot grill.

For peppermint & white chocolate brûlée, bring 350 ml (12 fl oz) double cream just to the boil in a saucepan, take off the heat and add 100 g (4 oz) good-quality white chocolate, broken into pieces, and leave until melted. Whisk the egg yolks with 25 g (1 oz) caster sugar, then gradually mix in the chocolate cream and the peppermint extract. Continue as above. Replace the raspberries with blueberries and serve as above.

Brandied Chocolate Fondue

Chocolate fondue – every chocolate lover's dream. This one delivers on rich chocolatey flavour, plus a delicious hint of brandy, but has the bonus of being lower in calories.

Serves 4
Preparation time 10 minutes
Cooking temperature high
Cooking time ¾–1 hour

100 g (3½ oz) dark chocolate,
  broken into pieces
6 tablespoons skimmed milk
1 teaspoon granular sweetener
1 tablespoon brandy

To serve
500 g (1 lb) strawberries,
  halved if large
150 g (5 oz) raspberries
1 large peach, halved, stoned
  and cut into chunks

Preheat the slow cooker if necessary. Place the chocolate, milk and sweetener in a heatproof bowl, cover with a saucer and stand in the slow cooker pot. Pour boiling water into the slow cooker pot to come halfway up the sides of the bowl, cover and cook on high for ¾–1 hour.

Remove the bowl from the slow cooker and stand on a large plate. Stir the fondue until smooth and glossy, then stir in the brandy.

Arrange the strawberries, raspberries and peaches on the plate. Serve with fondue forks or wooden skewers for spearing the fruit and dipping into the fondue.

For white chocolate fondue, place 100 g (3½ oz) white chocolate, broken into pieces, in a heatproof bowl with a few drops of vanilla extract and 6 tablespoons skimmed milk. Cook as above, then stir in 1 tablespoon Kirsch and serve with mixed berries.

Baked Honey & Orange Custards

Serves 4
Preparation time 15 minutes,
  plus cooling and chilling
Cooking temperature low
Cooking time 4–5 hours

2 eggs
2 egg yolks
400 ml (14 fl oz) semi-skimmed
  milk
3 teaspoons granular
  sweetener
3 teaspoons runny honey
½ teaspoon vanilla extract
finely grated rind of ½ orange,
  plus extra to garnish
large pinch of ground
  cinnamon

These no-guilt, low-cal custards with their sunshiny citrus flavour, plus a hint of honey and cinnamon, will brighten any grey day.

Preheat the slow cooker if necessary. Place the eggs, egg yolks and milk in a mixing bowl with the sweetener, honey and vanilla and whisk together until smooth. Strain the mixture through a sieve into a large jug, then whisk in the orange rind.

Divide the mixture between 4 x 150 ml (¼ pint) ovenproof dishes (checking first that the dishes fit in your slow cooker pot). Place the dishes in the slow cooker pot and sprinkle the cinnamon over the top. Pour hot water into the slow cooker pot until it comes halfway up the sides of the dishes. Cover the tops of the dishes with foil, place the lid on the slow cooker and cook on low for 4–5 hours until set.

Remove the dishes from the slow cooker and leave to cool. Transfer to the refrigerator to chill well before serving, garnished with a little extra orange rind.

For vanilla crème brûlée, follow the recipe above to cook and chill the custards, using 1 teaspoon vanilla extract and omitting the orange rind and cinnamon. Just before serving, sprinkle 1 teaspoon caster sugar over the top of each dish and caramelize the sugar with a cook's blow torch or under a preheated hot grill. Cool for a few minutes to allow the sugar to set hard, then serve with a few fresh raspberries.

Chocolate & Coffee Custard Creams

Coffee and chocolate are naturally delectable pairing and these rich little creams are a wonderful way to round off a special dinner, served with little macaroons, amaretti biscuits or wafers.

Serves 4
Preparation time 20 minutes, plus chilling
Cooking temperature low
Cooking time 3–3½ hours

450 ml (¾ pint) milk
100 g (3½ oz) plain dark chocolate, broken into pieces
1 teaspoon instant coffee
2 eggs
2 egg yolks
3 tablespoons light muscovado sugar
½ teaspoon vanilla extract
sifted cocoa powder, to decorate

For the topping
125 ml (4 fl oz) double cream
2 tablespoons light muscovado sugar
½ teaspoon vanilla extract

Preheat the slow cooker if necessary. Pour the milk into a saucepan and bring just to the boil. Remove from the heat, add the chocolate pieces and instant coffee and set aside for 5 minutes, stirring occasionally, until the chocolate has melted.

Put the whole eggs, egg yolks, sugar and vanilla extract in a bowl and whisk until just mixed. Gradually whisk in the hot chocolate milk until smooth. Strain through a sieve into the pan, then pour into 4 tall heatproof mugs, each 250 ml (8 fl oz), checking first that they will fit in the slow cooker pot.

Cover the tops of the mugs with foil and stand them in the slow cooker pot. Pour boiling water into the pot to come halfway up the sides of the mugs. Cover with the lid and cook on low for 3–3½ hours or until the custards are set and the tops can be lightly pressed with a fingertip.

Lift the mugs carefully out of the slow cooker pot using a tea towel. Leave to cool, then transfer to the refrigerator for at least 4 hours until chilled. Just before serving, whip the cream with the sugar and vanilla until soft swirls form. Spoon the topping over the custards and lightly dust with cocoa powder. Serve with dainty biscuits.

For vanilla custard pots, bring the milk just to the boil as above. Whisk the whole eggs and egg yolks with 2 tablespoons caster sugar and 1 teaspoon vanilla extract. Gradually whisk in the hot milk, then strain and continue as above, sprinkling the tops with a little grated nutmeg before cooking, if liked.

Plum & Blueberry Swirl

(GF) (L) (V)

A deliciously light way to end a meal, this low-cal dessert combines stewed fruit with citrus-scented Greek yogurt, and is a handy one as it can be made ahead and left in the refrigerator.

Serves 4
Preparation time 15 minutes, plus cooling and chilling
Cooking temperature high
Cooking time 2¼–2¾ hours

300 g (10 oz) ripe red plums, halved, stoned and cut into chunks
150 g (5 oz) blueberries
1 tablespoon granular sweetener
juice of ½ orange
3 tablespoons water
1 tablespoon cornflour

For the orange yogurt
200 ml (7 fl oz) fat-free Greek yogurt
finely grated rind of ½ orange
1 tablespoon granular sweetener

Preheat the slow cooker if necessary. Place the plums and blueberries in the slow cooker pot, sprinkle with the sweetener, then add the orange juice and measured water. Cover and cook on high for 2–2½ hours until the fruit is soft.

Mix the cornflour to a smooth paste with a little cold water and stir into the pot. Cover again and cook, still on high, for a further 15 minutes until thickened. Stir the fruit and leave to cool.

Mix the yogurt with the orange rind and sweetener. Divide the fruit between 4 serving glasses, top with the yogurt, then swirl together with a teaspoon. Chill until ready to serve.

For minted strawberry & blueberry swirl, place 300 g (10 oz) ripe strawberries, hulled, in the slow cooker pot with 150 g (5 oz) blueberries, 1 tablespoon granular sweetener and the juice of ½ orange. Cook as above, then thicken with the cornflour, cook for a further 15 minutes and leave to cool. Mix 200 ml (7 fl oz) fat-free Greek yogurt with 1 tablespoon chopped mint and 1 tablespoon granular sweetener, then swirl with the fruit as above.

Hot Toddy Clementines

Definitely one for the grown-ups, this dessert is blissfully easy to make and will fill the kitchen with a wonderful citrus aroma.

Serves 4
Preparation time 15 minutes
Cooking temperature low
Cooking time 2–3 hours

8 clementines

50 g (2 oz) honey

75 g (3 oz) light muscovado sugar

grated rind and juice of ½ lemon

4 tablespoons whisky

300 ml (½ pint) boiling water

15 g (½ oz) butter

Preheat the slow cooker if necessary. Peel the clementines, leaving them whole. Put the remaining ingredients in the slow cooker pot and mix together.

Add the clementines. Cover with the lid and cook on low for 2–3 hours or until piping hot. Spoon into shallow bowls and serve with just-melting scoops of vanilla ice cream.

For hot toddy apricots, put all the ingredients, omitting the clementines and sugar, into the slow cooker pot as above. Add 300 g (10 oz) ready-to-eat dried apricots and continue as above. Serve warm with crème fraîche or vanilla ice cream.

Raspberry & Rhubarb Oaty Crumble

Everyone loves crumble so this super-easy one with its flapjack and almond topping will go down a treat with friends and family.

Serves 4–5
Preparation time 15 minutes
Cooking temperature low
Cooking time 2–3 hours

400 g (13 oz) trimmed rhubarb
150 g (5 oz) frozen raspberries
50 g (2 oz) caster sugar
3 tablespoons water

For the topping
15 g (½ oz) butter
3 tablespoons flaked almonds
200 g (7 oz) ready-made
   flapjacks (about 4)

Preheat the slow cooker if necessary. Cut the rhubarb into 2.5 cm (1 inch) thick slices and add to the slow cooker pot with the still-frozen raspberries, the sugar and measured water. Cover with the lid and cook on low for 2–3 hours or until the rhubarb is just tender.

When almost ready to serve, heat the butter in a frying pan, add the almonds and crumble in the flapjacks. Fry, stirring, for 3–4 minutes or until hot and lightly browned. Spoon the fruit into bowls, sprinkle the crumble over the top and serve with thick cream.

For peach & mixed berry crumble, dice 3 fresh peaches, discarding the stones, and add to the slow cooker pot with 150 g (5 oz) mixed still-frozen summer fruits, the sugar and water as above. Cook and sprinkle with the flapjack topping as above.

Index